P9-DDS-796

MILLION DOLLAR MARKETING SECRETS

22 Top Pros Share Their Time-Tested Insights!

Million Dollar Marketing Secrets
22 Top Pros Share Their Time-Tested Insights!

Copyright © 2007 by JP Maroney. All rights reserved.

No part of this book may be used or reproduced in any manner whatsoever without written permission except in the case of brief quotations embodied in critical articles and reviews.

Maro©m

For information contact:
MAROCOM, LLC
Attn: Book Publishing Department
PO Box 9492
Tyler, Texas 75711-9492
1-800-304-5758
www.marocom.com

Books available for purchase in bulk quantities. Please contact Marocom at 1-800-304-5758 for more information.

ISBN 978-0-9704592-9-9
FIRST EDITION, 2007, Printed in Canada

ADDITIONAL BOOKS FROM MAROCOM™

Million Dollar Marketing Secrets
22 Top Pros Share Their Time-Tested Insights!

Million Dollar Marketing Secrets: Internet Edition (coming soon)
Top Pros Share Their Time-Tested Online Marketing Insights!

The Power To Achieve
10 Strategies For Personal And Professional Excellence!

The Service Path
Your Roadmap For Building Strong Customer Loyalty!

The Leadership Path
Your Roadmap For Leading People In The 21st Century!

The Productivity Path
Your Roadmap For Improving Employee Performance!

The Communication Path
Your Roadmap For Building Rapport And Getting Ideas Across!

The Wellness Path
Your Roadmap For Living Healthy And Feeling Great!

The Ultimate Contractor
Insider Secrets From Industry Leaders!

Gloria's Story

Check for additional titles online at
www.marocom.com/books

TABLE OF CONTENTS

TABLE OF CONTENTS

Success Starts Here...

Greetings Business Builder,

When I pulled together the 21 co-authors who joined me to write *Million Dollar Marketing Secrets*, I commissioned each with one objective; give their perspective on marketing by sharing their...

"Insider Secrets For Consistently, Effectively, and Profitably Marketing A Business!"

The result is a book that contains 22 distinct, yet complimentary perspectives on the topic of how to grow a business with effective marketing. The ideas, techniques, principles and strategies contained within the pages of this book include:

- How to Develop a Marketing Message That Connects With Your Best Prospects
- **7 Essentials for Increasing Sales**
- Turning ordinary ideas into extraordinary marketing
- **How to get valuable attention for your business**
- 9 Steps to Online Publicity
- **How to Brand Yourself and Your Business**
- Easy ways to turn freebies and give-a-ways into prospecting magnets
- **How to cultivate the right attitude for profitable** business networking
- **Steps to sucking massive profits from your client list**
- A little-known secret to outmaneuver the economy and make windfall profits year in and year out
- **Where and how to use testimonials**
- How to turn radio advertising into a sales booster
- **A secret tactic to ignite your advertising response**
- How to sell based on service - not price
- **The trick for tapping prospects' true buying motives**
- How to create a systematic sales and marketing process
- **Keys to placing your business at the top of prospects' minds at all times**
- How to incorporate gift cards into your marketing mix
- **Key to generating BIG returns on marketing investment**

- An underutilized marketing method that brings clients to you faster and more efficiently than traditional advertising
- **How to get more out of your business with less time**
- Insider strategies for yellow pages advertising
- **How to have fun AND make money too**
- Strategies for creating a lasting business brand
- **A simply way to stop prospects from price shopping**
- How turn an average business into extraordinary profits
- **And much, much more...**

If you want to go further, we've included contact information for each co-author on the first page of each chapter. Each co-author is a recognized expert, and most provide additional services like consulting, coaching, copywriting, speaking, and training.

Special Bonuses & Offers

Beginning on page 231, you'll find other resources available from our co-authors including: reports, newsletters, books, audio and video programs, assessment tools, and other training systems.

FREE... There's More Online At
www.MDMSbonus.com

Be sure to visit www.MDMSbonus.com and register to receive a "mega-pack" of FREE bonuses available exclusively to you as a reader of this book. I look forward to hearing your feedback regarding the additional tools and other resources.

On behalf of my team of co-authors and our publishing team at MAROCOM, I hope you find this book enlightening, inspiring, and highly useful in your quest to build your business.

Profitable Regards,

JP Maroney
Co-Author & Publisher

PS: Look for other titles available from MAROCOM at www.marocom.com/books

PPS: If you're interested in being considered as an author for one of our future projects contact us at info@marocom.com

STRATEGIC SERIES

FREE BONUSES

$367.00 in Marketing Reports, Templates, Worksheets, Tools and Training Included FREE with Your Book...

THE PRESSES HAVE STOPPED, BUT...

"YOUR MILLION DOLLAR MARKETING EDUCATION IS JUST STARTING...!"

I asked our group of co-authors, marketers and business builders to contribute because I knew every one of them had a wealth of experience to draw on.

My strategy was a deliberate one.

I wanted to expose you, the reader, to the broadest range of ideas I could... to stimulate you and show you there's an almost unlimited variety of ways for you to grow your business.

I knew my coauthors (and friends) would deliver. I think you'll agree they did just that. But they didn't stop there.

Even after the chapters were submitted and the proofs were approved, I received emails, faxes and phone calls letting me know they'd be happy to add even more content to a book already stuffed with powerful ideas.

In the past this would have been a real dilemma.

Because no matter how much we managed to put into a book like this, we have to leave even more out.

As passionate marketers, we were dismayed at the thought that no matter how well we covered a particular strategy or tactic, there was still a chance that you might want an opportunity to learn more. *So now, we're...*

(...continued on next page)

GOING BACK TO THE WELL...

I asked each of my co-authors to "go to the well" one more time to create something special for our readers. What they've dug up is nothing short of amazing.

If you look at the cover of your book -- or the header on the facing page -- you'll see that we mention $367.00 in FREE bonuses.

Well, the fact is...

IT'S A LIE!

The truth is... our co-authors have contributed FREE bonuses that FAR-EXCEED $367.00 in value. And... in fact, I held the number at $367.00 on the cover because I feared you would think it was too good to be true.

I kid you not -- You won't believe it until you personally claim your free bonuses provided by our co-authors. Here's how...

Go to www.MDMSbonus.com and claim your FREE bonuses at the special Million Dollar Marketing Secrets Bonus Page. You'll be taken to a members' only resource area with exclusive content available only to our readers.

You'll get:

FREE Reports...
FREE Marketing Checklists...
FREE Business-Building Templates...
FREE Training Videos...
FREE Audio Programs...
And much, much more...

It's all FREE -- FREE -- FREE (get the point?)

Claim Your FREE Bonuses At...
www.MDMSbonus.com

FREE!
Continue Your Learning And
Business-Building Online:
www.MDMSbonus.com

CHAPTER ONE

Never Sell Anything People Don't Want to Buy

How to Tailor Your Marketing to Connect With Your Client's Hidden Buying Triggers

Susan Adams

Author, Speaker & Consultant

"In many companies, marketing and sales rarely talk to each other," says Susan Adams. Ms Adams has successfully sold products and services for some of the world's best companies: GE, Pitney Bowes, and Bombardier Aerospace.

"In fact, you have sales people out talking to the customer every day and no one ever asks what the customers are talking about. Instead, they go hire consultants to 'talk to their customers. Because of this flawed approach, you don't get a marketing message that resonates with a prospect's hidden buying triggers."

Susan's 7 Suggestions:

- Business owner's need to be out talking to customers
- Tailor your marketing message to two or three benefits
- Get those benefits from your current customers
- Develop a Sales/Marketing swat team
- Meet monthly to discuss market conditions
- Make sure marketing campaigns match current customer's "hot buttons"
- Develop one message for sales and marketing

Susan Adams Consulting
Pittsburgh, PA • 412-422-1288 • www.SusanAdamsHome.com

Susan Adams

Never Sell Anything People Don't Want to Buy

How to Tailor Your Marketing to Connect With Your Client's Hidden Buying Triggers

There are many problems created in companies when marketing and sales aren't on the same page. Customers speak to sales people, but many times, marketing doesn't speak to sales. So, how is marketing developing a campaign that resonates with future customers when they don't know why current customers bought their products? I know what happens. Marketing prepares a "message" that doesn't connect with the prospects they're trying to reach.

In many companies, advertising agencies are creating the message that goes into newspaper ads, brochures and sales materials. How does a third party create a message that will resonate to your target market? In most instances, it doesn't. The best people in any company to develop the marketing message are those who passionately sell the product. In a small business, it's you, the owner. In a larger corporation it might be a collaborative effort between current customers, top sales people and marketing. If those who sell your product every day aren't involved in crafting your company's message, you'll miss out on the most important thing to your business-growing market share.

Your top sales people know why prospects are buying. They know the top three reasons prospects buy from your company. If those reasons aren't being used in your company brochure, be prepared for lackluster sales. Also, be prepared to spend a lot of time "weeding out tire kickers." If you're not reaching the right market for your product, your sales people will waste huge amounts of time sifting through unmotivated prospects looking for the one "hot lead."

I worked briefly for a company who had this marketing approach. You notice, I use the word briefly. For a sales professional, there is nothing more frustrating than spending endless hours on the phone with people who aren't real prospects. The company I'm speaking about sold 25 hour jet cards. The marketing director's thought was "quantity" not "quality." So, you have a product that only a very small segment of the market can afford, and you'd rather fill the database with a bunch of useless names. Management then assumes there's a problem in the sales force. After all, there were so many "leads" coming in. Those are inquiries, not leads. There's a huge difference.

As a business owner you need to develop the best strategy to find a marketing message that connects to the buyers you're trying to reach. If you can develop advertising that resonates with your target audience, you're now bringing in pre-qualified leads. These are not inquiries. If you're able to successfully develop this type of campaign, you've greatly increased the opportunity for increased sales.

HOW TO DEVELOP A MARKETING MESSAGE THAT CONNECTS WITH YOUR BEST PROSPECTS

Your marketing message should come from your best resource-the current customer. Why did they buy from you? Why do they like your product or service? What don't they like about your competitors? That may seem like an odd question. It's not. When I was selling fractional ownership of business jets, my largest competitor had a major flaw. Their sales people never talked about the great things their company did. They constantly did the "negative sell" against competitors. I had more customers tell me how turned off they were by the constant negative sales tactics. It always amazed me that a company that had so many good things to talk about spent their important face time with the customer bashing the competition.

Knowing that this type of buyer was put off by negative sales tactics is extremely important. This buyer wanted to be dealt with in a straightforward, honest manner. What if your advertising could incorporate some of this? Wouldn't it connect with your prospect?

See page 10 for exclusive reader-only FREE offers!

That's why it's critical to know your current customers. You need to know the following:

- Were their emotional reasons they bought your product?

- Did they buy because of price?

- What were the 3 things about your product/service that made them buy from you? In sales we call this the Value Statement.

- If they could change anything about your product or service, what would it be?

Emotional reasons can be difficult to dig out. For example, if I knew a prospect drove a fast car, then I knew I had a prospect who would "resonate" with the Learjet being a performance aircraft. The same is true for any business. You must find these hidden triggers that will draw a prospect to you for an emotional reason.

Price is always an interesting issue with current customers. What's important for you to know is do they see the value they're getting for the price they're paying. If not, you need to find out why. When prospects use the price objection during negotiations, it's not the price they're objecting to. It's the fact that they don't see value equal to that price. If your current customers feel they paid a fair price for what they received, then you have a good value proposition. A marketing campaign that draws the "best" buyers in as prospects will help your sale people sell your value proposition. In the end, attracting the right buyer will bring someone who understands your value proposition and is willing to pay top dollar for it. It will greatly eliminate the need for discounts. Something every business owner wants to hear!

The most difficult sales job I ever had was with a company that had little to no value proposition. I would sit in meetings and ask "Why would someone buy from us and not a competitor?" No one, not even the CEO, could answer me. It forced the sales force to constantly sell on price. You also don't get loyal customers. As soon as they find a comparable product at a lower price, they'll be gone. My advice to any company: Identify your value proposition and get it out there in your marketing materials.

Asking what they would change about your current product tells you why a competitor's message (and products) might eventually draw them away from you. If you know what they don't like, and can correct it, it's in your long term interest to do it. Or, survey other customers. If the same things keep coming up, you need to see how you can address their concerns. Your competitors know your weaknesses. And, they're probably talking to your customers constantly emphasizing the fact that you're not listening to their concerns.

You must know why your current customers would/wouldn't buy your product again. It's invaluable information.

WHO SHOULD DEVELOP YOUR MARKETING MESSAGE?

As I was writing this piece, I received one of Dan Kennedy's marketing email blasts. Ironically, it was about an experience he had when he was hired by Weight Watchers to beat the current control they were mailing. What did he do? He went to the two top sales people and asked them what they said to prospects to get them to buy. In all my years in sales, no one in marketing ever asked me why people were buying the product. Don't make the same mistake all the big companies make. Get sales actively involved in your message. You'll be happy you did.

Many companies also hire outside consultants to develop advertising campaigns. What does someone who doesn't work in your company possibly know about connecting with your customers? If you're looking for a message with no passion and a lot of "design" then hire someone outside your company. I saw a company I worked for stop doing all their advertising for 3-4 months while they waited for a "branding campaign" to be completed. Owners started calling me asking if we "were going out of business," because they hadn't see our ads in the Wall Street Journal. By time the "branding campaign" was finally finished, the damage had been done. The absence of advertising had competitors constantly calling our customers with rumors we were going out of business. Just as an aside, the campaign was a total bust. The message they developed didn't resonate with the target market. Instead of talking to customers, they spent their time in "concept meetings." All that money down the drain. Within 6 months, the campaign had been scrapped, and the old advertising resurrected.

See page 10 for exclusive reader-only FREE offers!

Even now, if you looked back at when this company started to lose market share, it can be directly tied to the 4 month period when advertising went dark. It's a critical lesson for any business owner.

Never let anyone who doesn't know you, your company or your customer tell you what the message should be. Get actively involved. The time it takes you will save untold number of dollars down the line.

HOW A WELL TARGETED MARKETING MESSAGE ACCELERATES THE BUYING PROCESS

Imagine your sales people have new prospects that have been efficiently weeded out through your improved marketing. Not just "inquiries," but true leads. Perhaps the buying cycle can be reduced by X number of days. In any company, one of the most frustrating things for sales management is sales forecasting. How do you speed up the buying process? How do you correctly forecast month to month sales numbers?

What if attracting better prospects speeds up the buying cycle? It has been my experience that most people buy in their time frame, not yours. If you know your prospect, you should know if they are motivated by something such as an End of the Quarter Special Offer. The point here is the prospect who contacted you because of your message is also a prospect who will move faster through the buying process.

This should also make sales forecasting easier. You know if your current customers were motivated by anything before they made a purchase. You know because you've already asked them this important question. You've also gained invaluable information about your value proposition. All these elements should attract better prospects who buy faster.

You also have the same message coming from marketing and sales. The prospect isn't getting one message in your marketing materials and a different message from your sales force. Through the course of my career, I don't know how many people I had call me and challenge a claim that was in marketing materials. Don't ever use "half-truths" or "over promise" in a brochure. Buyers aren't stupid. They'll eventually find out, and your sales people will waste time defending dubious statements rather than closing.

In summary, the more effective your marketing message, the better people you'll attract as potential customers. These higher quality prospects will resonate with the message they hear from your sales people and should be in the pipeline and closing faster. Because you now have the correct Value Proposition, you should also see less discounts.

THE 7 ESSENTIALS FOR INCREASING SALES THROUGH AN IMPROVED MARKETING MESSAGE:

1. Know your current customers

2. Have sales actively involved

3. Don't let anyone who doesn't know your customer prepare a marketing campaign

4. Marketing and sales should have the same Value Proposition

5. Understand the buying triggers for current customers

6. Develop a marketing campaign that resonates with the people you're trying to reach

7. Use these tips to shorten the sales cycle and improve forecasting

See page 10 for exclusive reader-only FREE offers!

FREE!
Continue Your Learning And
Business-Building Online:
www.MDMSbonus.com

CHAPTER TWO

e-Media Marketing

9 Steps to Online Publicity

Tom Antion

Internet Marketing Expert

Tom Antion is an Internet Marketing expert who actually makes money on the web.

He's been featured on major broadcast networks and print publications around the world including the Canadian Broadcast Network, The Australian Broadcast Network, The Tokyo Today show, INC. Magazine, four features in the Washington Post and hundreds of radio stations across the U.S.

He is the author of "How to Be a Kick Butt Publicity Hound" http://www.antion.com/publicityhound.htm.

Tom is a highly respected professional speaker who is a veteran of more than 2,100 paid presentations. He has helped thousands of other speakers, business presenters, executive and trainers learn how to be top platform performers. Tom is no deep theory guy. He teaches immediately usable techniques that anyone can learn to be great on stage -- and to get paid for it too.

Tom says, "No one ever lost credibility by being interesting." His "Wake 'em Up Speaking System" guarantees you will have the tools to keep your audience's attention from the moment you step on stage until your closing comments when they are begging for more.

Tom also publishes the largest electronic magazine in the world on public speaking with over 120,000 subscribers in 80 countries.

Antion & Associates
Virginia Beach, VA • 757-431-1366 • www.antion.com

Tom Antion

e-Media Marketing
9 Steps to Online Publicity

I've built my career on what I call "media marketing." Long before the Internet came along, I was on the radio, doing TV shows and writing and being written about in print publications. That's how I got all my work.

When your potential clients see you in the media it changes the balance of power in your favor when you are discussing working together. And guess what? Clients don't actually have to see you in the media for you to get the media advantage. When you have a good media hit you can brag about it forever.

A few years back I was asked by MSNBC to critique President Bush's presentation skills. I was on the air for no more than 3 minutes. Since the interviewer was long-winded himself, I bet I didn't say more than 15 words. Putting that appearance on my credential list closed a $15,000.00 job for me the next week and the people that paid me never saw me on the air.

Online publicity makes it even easier for you to spread your name around the world. Since the commercial Internet has come along, at least part of my business efforts have been geared toward making my name and websites show up online in as many places as possible. This makes my products and services rise in value and also makes it easier to sell them because many of the people buying have already heard of me.

HERE ARE 9 STEPS I USE REGULARLY TO BE SEEN ONLINE

1. Write and Distribute Articles

I don't want to hear the excuse, "I'm not good at writing," so I'm going to address that right now. You don't have to be good at writing to write articles. You can have articles that are perfect for the web written for you for as little as $3.00 each. I have a guy that's a little more Internet savvy write them for $5.00 a piece. . . .So where do you find these people?

Try: www.CraigsList.com
www.SoloGig.com
www.Elance.com
www.Writers-Editors.com

Why do I love articles so much and why have I put them as the first step? It's because articles give you a massive bang-for-your-buck. One article can be used in at least 11 ways.

You can use the same article:

- On your website

- In your electronic magazine (ezine)

- In your blog

- On other people's websites

- In other people's ezines

- In other people's blogs

- In article directories

- In traditional print periodicals

- As the basis for teleseminars and webinars

- In ebooks and printed books

- As press kit stuffers

- As product package stuffers

See page 10 for exclusive reader-only FREE offers!

Tip: When approaching other online or traditional publications, look at their "Editorial Calendars" first and pitch your article to appear in the month when they are already writing about your subject. This gives you a much greater chance to get in. Pitch well in advance of the month when they are covering your topic.

Additional Resources:
http://www.GreatInternetMarketing.com/publicity.htm

2. Do Online Press Releases

Learn to write a press release and distribute it at online press release services. There are many places that will teach you how to write a release. Try www.publicityhound.com or you can use the same resources above that you used to find article writers.

I did a press release recently on one of my golf sites www.GolfArticles.net . It took about 10 minutes to write and it got 230,000 reads in the first week.

Many of the Press Release companies below have free and paid services. The more you pay, the more they distribute your release. Give the free ones a shot until your press release writing skill improves and then graduate to the paid services on your most important releases. Some of them will help you write the release or write it for you for a fee.

www.PRWeb.com
www.PRWebDirect.com
www.ExpertClick.com/
www.Free-Press-Release.com
http://I-NewsWire.com/
www.PressReleaseNetwork.com

3. Get listed in directories

Get your website listed in directories. Note: a directory is not a search engine. They are different animals. In a directory, a real person looks at your website and decides if it is good enough to be in their directory and also where it belongs in the directory.

The main directory you want to get in is www.Dmoz.org. You probably never heard of it, but if you get in DMOZ AKA "The open directory project," your site will show up in many other search facilities around the world. Also, getting in Dmoz will make your site look much better to the regular search engines.

Getting links from many of the smaller directories will probably help you out in the long run. Here's a service that will submit your site to several hundred directories.

www.directoriessubmission.com

4. Optimize your website

High rankings in search engines can bring you enormous amounts of traffic and they don't come by accident. You need to learn how to place keywords on your webpages so that when the search engine comes looking for pages about a certain topic, your site comes up high in the search results.

I don't use an expensive search engine optimization firm for this. I simply make many pages based on the same keyword and I put that keyword (or keyword phrase) a reasonable amount of times on each of the pages. I also make each website all about one topic and I try to get people to link "to" my site without giving up a link "out" of my site.

Of course, there are a few more details to this method, but if you learn this, you will either be able to get high rankings yourself, or you can hire high school kids to make pages for you rather then paying 1000.00 a day for a fancy search engine optimization firm.

Resource http://www.antion.com/click.htm

5. Get mentioned

Even if you aren't the featured person in a story there are ways to increase the perception that you are "everywhere."

One method is to find and get to know people who are writing about your topic. This used to be quite a task and now you can do it with no sweat at all right from your desktop.

Visit one or all of the major online news sites like:
www.news.google.com
http://news.search.yahoo.com
www.topix.net

See page 10 for exclusive reader-only FREE offers!

Type your topic into their search box(s). You will bring up articles in the news about that topic and all you have to do is note the author of the article. Do this for a week or two and you'll know all the major players who are writing about your topic regularly. Start contacting them with praise, comments, and offers to be a resource and soon comments by you will be plastered all over your target market.

Forthcoming Books

Also check your library for a copy of "Forthcoming Books." Use this book to find out about books in your field that have not yet been released. You can contact the author directly and offer to do peer reviews or add content to the book in exchange for a mention in the book.

Letters to the Website/Blog Editor

Whenever you see a website or blog that has an article about your topic, you can always write to the website owner or editor and comment on the article. This gives a link back to your website and also helps establish you as an expert in the field.

> Tip: a way to keep up with what is going on in your industry is to sign up for free accounts at Google Alerts www.google.com/alerts Put in keywords that you want info on and any time that keyword shows up in the news Google will email you.

6. Do teleseminars

Offer to be a guest on teleseminars in your field or in front of a complimentary target audience. You can find many teleseminars by simply going to Google and typing in "teleseminars", or "teleclasses" followed by your topic.

7. Publish an electronic magazine

This tip got me a 100K contract for part time work. When you build up a big database of people that hear from you regularly you just never know who is on the list.

I had a subscriber that was a columnist for a major newspaper. She called to ask me a question and she printed my answer in her column. At the same time a PR firm that was hired by CBS was looking for a spokesperson for a major website they owned. They wanted a credible Internet marketer who was good at public speaking. They read her column that was quoting me.

I got a contract worth $100,000.00 for
about 30 days of part time work.

Publishing an ezine is not really novel nowadays, but it is still a way to prove your expertise and spread your name around the world.

8. Publish a blog

There are many good reasons to start a blog. For those of you that don't know, a blog is simply a specialized kind of website that doesn't really need a web designer and is expected to be updated frequently with relatively small postings.

Why should you bother?

- Search engines love the postings.

- You can link it to your main website(s) for extra traffic.

- If someone subscribes to your blog, you don't have to worry about email filters stopping your message from getting through.

- It keeps you producing new content regularly. (some people compile all their little postings into one place and get a book or ebook out of it)

- They are free or really cheap to start and operate.

Visit www.blogger.com (owned by Google) and start a free blog right now. If you don't like it, delete it and start another one.

Have fun with it. For a sample visit one of my blogs www.GreatPublicSpeaking.blogspot.com

Tips: Put your best keywords in the titles of your postings and when you make a posting to your blog visit www.pingomatic.com Tell them about your posting and they will alert the major blog directories that you have updated your blog.

See page 10 for exclusive reader-only FREE offers!

9. Internet Radio

Is anyone listening to Internet Radio? . . . Well, not like they listen to regular radio. Most of the publicity you'll get from Internet radio will come over time as people listen to the replays. This is a major advantage over traditional radio shows in that your interview lives on forever. Some hosts will give you the recording and allow . . . even encourage you to turn it into a product. . . . Radio show hosts are publicity hounds too!

To find shows you can be interviewed on type "Internet Radio" into Google and you'll find thousands of listings.

There you have it. I've built a multi-million dollar business out of the nine steps above. Don't forget though, unless you're just an ego freak when you get traffic and get known on line, you must turn it in to cash which is another topic altogether.

See you on the web.

Get More...

See page 230 for special offers and other
information from our co-authors!

FREE!

**Continue Your Learning And
Business-Building Online:
www.MDMSbonus.com**

CHAPTER THREE

FREE SEX
(aka: No Rules...Just Results)

**How to Break Away from Your Competitors
with Outside-The-Box Marketing Tactics**

Jack Bastide

*Copywriter, Speaker &
Marketing Consultant*

Jack "Outside the Box Bastide" is a marketing consultant, best-selling author, captivating speaker, professional copywriter, hard-core entrepreneur and a partridge in a pear tree. Since the age of 7 he has been involved in numerous businesses, made a lot of money, lost a lot of money, and learned a lot along the way.

Jack's entrepreneurial career started with selling painted seashells as a child. He has owned several distribution routes, a grocery store, and a boutique. He has been involved in Network Marketing, invested in Real Estate, mail-order, franchises and anything else you can think of.

Jack's informative articles have appeared in numerous offline and online publications. He is well-known and respected on several online marketing forums. He has his own Network Marketing resource site and forum at HowToMLM.com

Jack is also a world class copywriter. He has written copy for some of the top names in the business as well as for his own projects. His no-nonsense style has produced Kick-Ass results for himself and his clients. His sales copy isn't cheap ... but it's worth it.

Jack is a big believer in joint ventures and strategic alliances. He has arranged numerous profitable JV's through his website JvWithJack.com

Honest Ventures, Inc.
Orlando, FL • 1-800-595-2252 • www.JackBastide.com

Jack Bastide

FREE SEX
(aka: No Rules...Just Results)

How to Break Away from Your Competitors with Outside-The-Box Marketing Tactics

This chapter has nothing to do with sex ... and everything to do with marketing! The term "Free Sex" is a metaphor for Provocative (Attention Getting) Marketing Techniques. There is a reason that I call it "Free Sex." It relates back to a story from my college days. More on that later ...

I bet you scanned through the table of contents in this book and came here first. C'mon admit it! The title got your attention. By using attention getting techniques like this in your business, you will stand out from your competition, attract more customers, and crush your competition!

"Research in psychology has shown that novel, emotion-evoking stimuli attract a person's attention. It has the same effect for advertising. Provocative images and words are more likely to be noticed by a potential consumer. Subsequently, the attention directed toward the ad may enhance the probability the ad's message is processed."- Tom Reichert USA Today May 2001

This chapter is not about using sex in advertising. It's about how to make your business get noticed. Know your market, see what your competition is doing and push the envelope as far as possible without offending your target audience. Do it right and your business will prosper.

A QUICK WORD OF CAUTION:
KNOW YOUR MARKET...AND YOUR COMPETITION

Several years ago Calvin Klein created a lot of controversy by running ads with underage models in provocative poses. He later had to pull the ads. Before he pulled them he got a lot of attention and a lot of business. Calvin is in the fashion industry. Would those ads have worked if he ran a funeral parlor or a law firm? Probably not. Calvin knew his market.

What is acceptable in one market may be going overboard in another. If you are in the used car business you can get away with perching bikini clad models on the hood of you product ... but what if you sell caskets? A good way to determine what you can get away with is to see what your competition is doing. Keep a close eye on what they are doing ... and go a little beyond that.

"FREE SEX" ... HOW IT STARTED

It all started back in college. Our fraternity advertised our parties by posting flyers on campus. There were at least 10 other fraternities doing the same thing. We would usually get about 80 - 100 people at our parties, instead of the 200 that we wanted to get. In order to do better we needed a way to stand out from our competition (the other fraternities) and get attention.

Most of the party flyers looked the same. Ours had to be different. I changed the headline from **"Fraternity Party"** to **"Free Sex."** I left the rest of the flier unchanged. My fraternity bothers thought I was crazy! When the night of the party came, instead of the usual 80 - 100 guests, we had over 400! The headline change resulted it a 400% increase in business!

This was my first experience with the power of provocative marketing. A simple headline change resulted in a huge increase of business. Since then I have used provocative marketing many times and gotten great success for myself and my clients.

SICKOFTHEBOSS.COM

One provocative marketing campaign that I used personally with great success was my Sick of the Boss campaign. I got the idea one day when I saw a guy handing out flyers that said "Work At Home." Since I was also involved in a "Work at Home" business I wanted to do something similar. It had to be different enough to attract attention.

I needed a new angle. I came up with the tagline **"Sick of the Boss?"** I made up some flyers and a sign that said Sick of the Boss? I stood on a busy corner with the flyers. The reaction was amazing! People were smiling at me and practically attacking me to get a flier! I set up a website on the domain SickOfTheBoss.com ... It was very popular.

One day my boss saw me doing this. Later that day he called me to his office. I thought I was going to get fired. It turned out he was sick of his boss and wanted to know what I was doing! I took the common "Work at Home" theme and gave it a new angle. The rest is history!

P.T. BARNUM - THE FATHER OF PROVOCATIVE MARKETING

Phineas Taylor Barnum was born at Bethel, Connecticut in 1810. A master showman, he called himself the Prince of Humbug ... I like to think of him as the father of provocative marketing. One of his first stunts was when he moved to NYC and exhibited a black woman as George Washington's nurse. He claimed she was 161 years old. She was actually half that age.

Other stunts included a phony mermaid, the original bearded lady, the legitimate midget General Tom Thumb, the "Swedish Nightingale" Jenny Lind, and other crowd pleasers before starting his circus. I highly recommend that you read any literature you can find on this marketing genius.

SEXY MARKETING

Although this chapter is not specifically about sex in advertising, here are a couple of sexy ads that got a lot of attention. They created controversy and brought the companies using them a lot of business.

Brooke Shields And Her Jeans - In 1980, 15 year old model Brooke Shields was cast in several provocative Calvin Klein Jeans ads. In one of the ads the camera panned slowly across her body while she uttered the now famous line, "Do you want to know what comes between me and my Calvins? ... Nothing." People are still talking about it over 25 years later!

Jenny McCarthy Candies Ad - a former model and playboy bunny, Jenny is probably best known for the ad she did for Candies Shoes in February 1997. The ad showed Jenny on the toilet, panties down, legs akimbo, wearing only Candies shoes. Although the camera angle didn't show anything, the ensuing attention turned into tons of free publicity for the shoe company.

TURNING THE ORDINARY
INTO THE EXTRAORDINARY

With my Sick of the Boss campaign I took the very ordinary "Work at Home" theme and created an angle that resonated with people and got attention. Here are a couple of examples of taking products that were quite ordinary and giving them a new "spin."

Sea-Monkeys - Sea-Monkeys began "life" in the 1960's, invented by Harold von Braunhut. You may remember them for the advertisements found in comic books of the 60 - 70's. These were actually tiny brine shrimp that came to life when water was added.

Billions of the tiny creatures have been sold over the years and have generated fan websites, a television series, and a video game. Astronaut John Glenn took 400 million "Amazing Sea-Monkeys" into space with him in 1998.

The Pet Rock - This was a 1970's fad created by advertising executive Gary Dahl. They were ordinary gray pebbles bought at a builders supply store and marketed as if they were live pets. The fad lasted only about six months, ending with the Christmas season in December 1975; but in its short run, the Pet Rock made Dahl a millionaire.

These are two perfect examples of what can be done when you have a marketing mindset. If somebody can take mundane products like brine shrimp eggs or rocks and make them exciting and interesting, imagine what you can do with your product or service!

LOCAL MERCHANTS GET PROVOCATIVE

You don't have to have a large budget and do national advertising to get attention. Here are some local merchants that created (or are still creating) attention by thinking out of the box.

See page 10 for exclusive reader-only FREE offers!

Crazy Eddie

Crazy Eddie was a consumer electronics chain which was started in the 1970's in Brooklyn, NY, by businessman Eddie Anta. The chain was well known for its television and radio commercials in which Actor Jerry Carroll always ended his sales pitch with the memorable tag-line "Crazy Eddie - His Prices Are In-saaane."

The Crazy Eddie character was so popular that it was later parodied in the popular TV Series "Futurama" and a Weird Al Yankovic Video. One of his commercials is featured in the movie "Splash" with Tom Hanks. To this day there are Crazy Eddie tribute pages on the internet and people trade Crazy Eddie shirts and other memorabilia on Ebay.

"I Buy Rolexes" Truck on I-4

Today I was driving to a meeting with one of my clients on I-4, a major interstate here in Central Florida. While driving, I noticed a truck parked in a field on the side of the road. The reason I noticed it was because on the side of the truck it said "I BUY ROLEXES" in huge letters with a phone number.

This achieved the same effect of one of those roadside billboards — only 10 times more powerful. Why was it more powerful? It was different and stood out. I must have passed hundreds of billboards on my drive. I don't remember them … I remember the truck.

Morgan and Morgan Law Firm

This is a very successful law firm in Central Florida. If you're anywhere in the Orlando area, you can't help but see one of their commercials on TV or their roadside billboards promoting their website.

No offense to attorneys, but most attorneys have no clue when it comes to marketing. The fact that M&M is doing any marketing at all is putting them way ahead of the competition and allowing them to dominate their local market.

There was a recent story in the Orlando Sentinel where other attorneys were complaining that all the M&M advertising didn't look professional. My advice to the other attorneys? "Looking professional" isn't going to pay your bills. M&M is making a fortune.

What creative thing can you do with your business to get noticed? Remember: See what your competition is doing … and do a little more (If you're an attorney that's not difficult!)

HOW CAN I GET ATTENTION
FOR MY BUSINESS?

We have spoken a little about provocative marketing. I have given you some examples of things I have done. I have shown you some things that others have done. So now the question is "What can you do?"

Here are some things that you can implement in your business immediately:

An Unusual Business Card

A great way to stand out from your competition is to have an unusual business card. For my own business card I took a picture of my dog "Puffin" lying on a surfboard in the pool. On his back is perched one of my lovebirds. When I call people they always say "Oh you're the guy with the dog on his business card." I have helped many of my clients create killer business cards.

Yellow Pages Ads

A prime candidate for provocative advertising is the yellow pages. Many businesses are spending hundreds, if not thousands, of dollars for large ads and getting meager results. Many yellow pages ads don't even have a headline! By using a little imagination you can dominate the yellow pages in your area.

Recently I was looking for a plumber. I picked up the yellow pages and there were several pages of ads that all looked alike. One ad was a little bit different. It had a headline that said "My Plumber Will Smell Good and Show Up On Time Or I'll Pay You!!" I called the guy. As advertised, he showed up on time and happily took my $653.18!

Join a Network Marketing Company

Network Marketing, Multi-Level Marketing, MLM. Call it what you want. Love it or hate it. These people know how to market! I have spent over 10 years in this industry. It's where I honed many of my provocative attention-getting marketing techniques. People in the Network Marketing industry don't have large advertising budgets to throw away on ineffective advertising. Join a Network Marketing Company ... It's a great way to learn.

See page 10 for exclusive reader-only FREE offers!

Be a Local Celebrity

Here in Orlando there is a chain of appliances stores called "Appliance Direct." They're growing like wildfire and much of this can be attributed to their wacky commercials. They buy time on cable TV and have two spokespeople. One is a lady who wears a bright green fluorescent dress. The other is an Asian guy who tells funny stories about appliances.

Appliance Direct had a booth at a recent home show at the Orange County Convention Center here in Central Florida. While many exhibitors were twiddling their thumbs, the Appliance Direct booth was mobbed... Why? The Green dress lady was handing out t-shirts and giving autographs! **You can be the green dress lady for your market.**

Brand Yourself and Your Business

You don't just want to be "A Realtor", or A "Mortgage Broker" , or "An Attorney". Why not take a picture of yourself playing guitar and brand yourself as the Rockin' Realtor? Put it on all your promotional materials. Be the person that your target audience thinks of when they need your service ... Brand yourself!

Be Known as an Expert in Your Field

One way to stand out from your competition is to become known as an expert in your field. You can write informative articles for local publications in your area. Are you an insurance agent? Write some articles on different types of insurance. You may also want to consider becoming a semi-regular columnist in a local paper.

Publicity Stunts

A great way to get attention is through the use of publicity stunts. A master at this is Alan Abel who bills himself as a "professional hoaxer" and with good reason.

Here is some of his work:

1990 - Lottery Hoax: Alan hired actress Lee Chirillo to pose as the winner of the $35 Million Dollar Lottery. In order to attract the media, Alan and a group of his pranksters staged a lavish party at the Omni Park Plaza Hotel in mid-town Manhattan and threw dollar bills out the window. When the news got out that an attractive single woman had won a fortune in the state lottery, reporters were all over the story.

1997- Jenny McCarthy: In the aftermath of a controversial ad for Candie's shoes, featuring Jenny McCarthy sitting on a toilet, a man named Stoidi Puekaw decided to market "Jenny's Pint O' Pee" worldwide. He claimed that there was a warehouse filled with 500,000 cases of her urine stored in Mexico, packaged and ready for shipping.

McCarthy's lawyers quickly drafted a cease and desist letter, claiming trademark infringement. When it was revealed that it was a joke, Stoidi Puekaw (Abel) pointed out that the lawyers should have read his name backwards (Wake Up Idiots!).

> You can read more about Alan Abel at:
> http://www.AlanAbel.com

Abel's stunts are admittedly quite elaborate. What can you do in your business? Let's say you are a realtor. What if you leaked a story to the local press that while showing a house you discovered $10,000,000 in the closet? Think that might get you some attention?

Publicity stunts are not for everybody, but if you've got the guts to use them, they can really pay off! Remember ... There is no such thing as bad publicity!

FREE SEX – AND MY WIFE!

Well it's about that time. I have only been allotted a certain amount of words for this chapter. I have already gone over that amount. There is so much more to say .... I hope you enjoyed this chapter on provocative marketing. When I first gave it to my wife to proofread, the first thing she said was "Free Sex? What the heck is that?" I guess this just proves the fact that provocative marketing really works!

FREE!

Continue Your Learning And
Business-Building Online:
www.MDMSbonus.com

CHAPTER FOUR

Million Dollar Networking Strategies to Grow Your Business

High-Leverage Secrets to Add Value to Every Moment Of Your Networking Experience

Andy and Shawn Catsimanes

Copywriters and Consultants

Andy and Shawn Catsimanes publish the monthly Ezine, "The Corporate Muse."

As marketers and direct response copywriters, with backgrounds in business-to-business sales and writing fiction, they understand the limitless power of networking. Through networking they've made invaluable friendships and alliances with a number of influential people. Many are mentioned here in this chapter.

In this chapter you'll learn:

- The real meaning of networking
- The best ways to approach someone new
- Tips that will make you memorable
- Steps to a more effective networking experience
- Networking venues you might never have envisioned
- Valuable follow-up techniques to keep your connections strong
- Some of the most powerful networking secrets from some of the most powerful networking gurus

QuickSilver CopyWriters

Overland Park, KS • 1-888-733-0326 • www.quicksilvercopywriters.com

Andy and Shawn Catsimanes

Million Dollar Networking Strategies to Grow Your Business

High-Leverage Secrets to Add Value to Every Moment Of Your Networking Experience

For years, I had the wrong idea about networking. Mention the word and I cringed. I pictured - walk into a big room full of strangers, introduce myself to people who won't remember my name, and hand them my business card. No thank you.

Then I discovered the power center of networking: making new friends. Or as one friend put it, "I just show up and talk to people." I can do that. You can too. If you decide before attending the next seminar or posting on the next forum or showing up at the next networking function that you are there to meet people and discover what you can do for them, your fears will dissipate.

That's networking in a nutshell. Sounds too simple, doesn't it? No matter what you've been told, networking is a very basic human experience. We're all social creatures by nature. We want and need people around us. We network every day; we just don't call it that. So why when it becomes an organized networking event, do we twist it into something it isn't and revert back into ourselves?

Good questions and I will try to answer them, but I can't do it without help. In preparation for this chapter, I surveyed 18 super-successful networkers. While much of what you'll hear may sound similar, it's great to see different approaches. By reading carefully, you should be able to find one that will work for you. Let me take a moment here to thank all our contributors for their generosity, openness and willingness to share.

Enjoy their wisdom!

WHAT IS NETWORKING ANYWAY?

Maybe we should begin with what we mean by networking. Accomplished copywriter and business builder Ray Edwards (www.rayedwards.com) defines it this way: "In the business sense, usually we mean - the ability to meet people to know them and to get access to their knowledge, their skills, their network of contacts or their ability to get certain things done." But that doesn't mean using people. Instead he says, "If when you meet people, you will work hardest to be of value to them, all the benefits of networking, as we mean them, will naturally flow from that relationship."

Ray cautions against getting "caught up with techniques, tools and systems of how to network." Instead he recommends being nice and talking to anyone within three feet of you. "Because you never know who a person is or what they're about or in what way you can contribute to them and vice versa, until you take the trouble to get to know them a little bit."

Top copywriting coach David Garfinkel, (www.copynewsletter.com) agrees. "A lot of people think networking is this formal process with checklists and canned phrases that you use. To me, it's not … at the most fundamental level I think networking is being interested in other people and talking to them."

If, like David, you are "endlessly curious about people," you'll find out just how interesting they can be. Look for subjects you share in common. And for ideas that are different. Either can spark conversation.

Next time you attend a networking event, take along David's sage advice: "Go in with the entrepreneurial spirit of giving and when you meet someone; think, what can we do together, rather than what can you do for me. You'll actually have a better time. You'll end up with more. And you'll be more welcomed into different opportunities."

CULTIVATING THE RIGHT ATTITUDE

The one thing I heard more often than anything else is - make it about the other person. You have to go with the outlook of being helpful and willing to give. Two of the savviest marketers we know, Michel and Sylvie Fortin (www.contextcash.com) gave great advice on this subject. "The first rule of networking is being ready to help first before asking for a single thing," says Sylvie.

Michel stresses this point, "Don't think of how it can benefit you. Think of how you can be a benefit to someone else. Show genuine interest in the other person ... be interested, rather than trying to be interesting. It will serve you well."

When I asked about attending events together, they said they each have a unique following and often separated to network more effectively. Later, they compare notes. Michel says, "We often see how we can exchange contacts. We can bring together people from individual groups. The separation allows dual impact." Frequently, they unite people who wouldn't have been able to connect on their own.

If you want to make an impact at a seminar, you need to develop the proper perspective. Be careful not to miss opportunities by setting your sights on the "gurus." Get to know the people sitting around you. Mingle. Socialize. Talk to everyone. If that intimidates you, look at it like Sylvie does: "We're all in the same boat. We're just in different levels of the boat. If you think that way, you'll begin to realize the possibilities are limitless."

STEPS TO A SUCCESSFUL
NETWORKING EXPERIENCE

"The first and most important is to focus on them. If you approach it with - Me, Me, Me - it's a recipe for failure," says copywriter and web marketing strategist Leah Carson (www.catalystcopy.com). "By focusing on them, you relieve the pressure on yourself."

Listening is the second step. To effectively listen, Leah advises, "Don't rehearse in your mind the pitch that you're going to give them. Don't look to the next target or next comment ... ask questions. It's the simplest way to focus." And then, listen to their answers - you'll be amazed at what you'll learn.

The third step is to offer something of value. "Look for an opportunity to do something they'll really remember and appreciate and will set you apart from all the people you're talking to."

Ultimately, she says, "Money's important, but human connection is what most of us are after."

Writer and business builder Eileen Coale (www.eileencoale.com) looks for a feeling of good will when approaching other networkers. "We might have nothing to offer each other right now, but if we keep in touch, we can be a resource down the line for each other." To keep her name on their minds, she invites them to sign up for her monthly ezine.

Another effective method she uses, she learned from a prominent marketer. "If you're reading something and it makes you think of somebody that you met. Clip it and send it to them with a little sticky note."

Before Eileen began her business, she was quite shy. She found a quote in a book that helped overcome her nervousness, "Act like a host, not a guest ... Anytime I don't feel confident, I start pretending I'm the host and introducing people and introducing myself and it works."

TRICKS OF THE TRADE

Perhaps some of the most unique tips to ensure you leave a memorable impression came from marketer and copywriter Ryan Healy (www.healymarketing.com). One of his favorites is "mirroring" the other person's body movements. "Tilting your head when they tilt their head. Crossing your arms when they cross their arms ... it creates a connection between you and the person you are talking to ... they don't even know it's going on ... all of a sudden, they get a good feeling about you. They think, Oh he's like me. That's what it's really all about - getting people to know, like and trust you."

Another way Ryan gets in the door with people is by purchasing their products. "If you want to gain access to people and to what they have access to, you need to be willing to invest in the relationship before they even know who you are. A conscious decision I've made is to spend my money with people I want to become connected with. And not necessarily because they have the potential to send me work, but because they have the potential to recommend me or refer me."

Business growth strategist Mike Morgan (www.outsource-copy.com) has three rules when attending seminars. First, "Be open at all times." His openness led him to a $25,000 paycheck.

His second rule: "Really focus in on your prospect and what they need and listen well." There's no substitute for listening. He adds, "You have to fully understand their needs before you can offer any solutions."

"One of the primary things I look for is - we call them buying signals in selling. Those can be questions like … when do you think you can fit me in? Or when can we talk more?"

Mike says learning to recognize these signs is a skill most people can learn.

Rule # 3: Set goals before attending a seminar. He says to focus on every aspect of what you want to accomplish, from how many people you plan to talk to each day, to how you'll spend your time. "Focus on the outcome." It will reduce your fears.

According to Dr. Harlan Kilstein, an extraordinary mentor and phenomenal copywriter, (www.sixfigurecopy.com), to be successful, you must, "Change your entire orientation from what's in it for me, to what can I do for them? If someone's going there to get someone's business, they probably have zero chance of succeeding. If on the other hand, you say, how can I enhance this person's business - that will go a long way."

It's easy to get intimidated by people you think of as important, but Dr. Kilstein says, "These people are human. These people are approachable … if you see me at a seminar, don't be afraid to walk up and say, 'Hi.'"

Dr. Kilstein offers this last piece of advice: "Don't go into hock to go to seminars. Save money with a specific purpose in mind. People who encourage you to go into debt to attend, say it's based on potential - it's based on a lie."

OPPORTUNITIES ARE ALL AROUND YOU

Be careful not to get caught up in thinking the only places to network are organized events or forums. Those are just the beginning. Stretch your imagination to include any place you're involved with other people.

Consider these examples Ellen Violette, "The eBook Coach," (www.theebookcoach.com) gave me, "I was in a coaching class when I first started and the coach had a mastermind group. It was really powerful. And now I have a couple for my classes - I've created the eBook Profit Writers Club. I think it's actually the only one where people can come and just mastermind - get feedback on their titles, their chapter headings, whatever it is they're working on … I'm a firm believer in mastermind groups, because then it's people working together."

She added, "The way networking is now with the Internet, to me, joint venturing is networking." Joint venturing introduces you to new people through teleseminars and becoming a part of each other's lists. There are myriad ways it creates associations for you and whomever you JV with.

If you're not familiar with BNI, it stands for Business Network International. There are 4,175 chapters in 26 countries. You can find out more at: www.bni.com.

Jason Shields of S & H Lifetime Planning is the president of one of the local chapters. BNI groups gather once a week for the sole purpose of generating referrals. Only one person from each profession is allowed per chapter, giving you an opportunity to build relationships outside your own line of work.

"The number one reason to join a BNI Chapter is to grow your business," Jason says, "If the chapter is working like it should, approximately 50% of your business should come from your BNI connections."

"Visit several," Jason concludes, "All of them have a different purpose. Shop around and find one that fits your needs ... BNI's policy allows anyone to attend two meetings before you have to make a commitment or pay any dues. Take advantage of that."

NETWORKING ON FORUMS

Copywriter Gary Glasscock (www.gc-copywriting.com) approaches all of his networking venues with the position of - What knowledge do I have to offer? Although he attends seminars, he's more familiar with forums.

Forums are generally easy to join. If you want, you can remain a lurker on the periphery, but the true value is found in participation. It helps ease the isolation of many Internet-based businesses and puts you smack in the middle of a group of your peers.

Gary says it's important to post fairly consistently. "Let people know you're there to help ... you've got to be willing to give before you can ask anything from a forum. If you don't go with that attitude, then I don't believe you'll have much success at all."

"If you have any fears about anything, do your best to put those aside," Gary suggests, "Jump into the fray and do it ... that's the only way you're going to profit from any of it."

See page 10 for exclusive reader-only FREE offers!

REMEMBER - RELATIONSHIPS
TAKE TIME TO BUILD

Like fine wine and cheese, relationships can't be rushed. Developing worthwhile ones, means investing your time and your knowledge.

"Internet Marketing Sweetie," Alice Seba (www.aliceseba.com) agrees: "I think patience is important. Things aren't going to happen overnight." She says people who push to promote their products could see results, but she doesn't recommend it.

When at seminars or on forums, Alice says, "I position myself as unassuming … I want to talk, share ideas with people. Start to know the people I could work with and do projects with. There's no pitching for me. No expectations from people.

See where I might help them out, do something for them, and go from there … start to think about what you can do for the community and it all comes back to you."

THE POWER OF FOLLOW-UP

"Make sure that you follow up with closer connections," says "Accidental Millionaire" Stephanie Frank (www.accidentalmillionaire.com). "Have little thank you cards close by.

Make yourself memorable. People are more likely to remember you after the event."

She doesn't recommend following up with everybody. "A lot of times people can fall into the maybe someday category … when you come out of an event, you should have a handful of people who are going to help you right now.

And a handful or maybe you have a pocketful or bagful of information from people who you want to get to know better in the future."

Stephanie sends personal notes for the hot people. For the not-so-hot people she liked, but isn't sure how they would fit, she says, "We have an email that we send inviting them to receive a free gift."

When it comes to follow-up, business coach Alan Boyer (www.leaders-perspective.com) leads the way. In fact, I asked him to participate in the survey specifically because of how well he followed up with me after I'd visited his site.

Alan's developed a Four-Step Follow-Up System:

1) Send them an email, mentioning something they said that either caught your attention, or seemed important to them. (He frequently passes on a contact that would be beneficial to them based on something they said.)

2) Set an appointment to talk further. (Try for: three days after the event.)

3) Seek a second appointment.

4) Ask if they'd like to be on your email list of hints and tips to double your business.

And if they eventually fall out the of the loop, don't be afraid to ask if they'd like to remain on your email list. Alan does this and says most do. It gives him exposure for months to come.

THE BEGINNING

If you've never attended a seminar or joined a forum, there's no better time than the present. You could be missing a wealth of contacts and information.

Like successful affiliate marketers Cynthia and Larry Denton (www.elfincorp.com) said, "You can always learn something. Step up to the plate - don't be hesitant about asking questions and be willing to participate and learn. Don't let the knowledge you have prevent you from getting more. It's what you learn after you know it all, that really matters."

As my wise colleagues all told me, Just do it. You never know who you'll meet, how the two of you might fill a mutual need, or maybe just make a new friend for life. And what could be better than that?

FREE!
Continue Your Learning And
Business-Building Online:
www.MDMSbonus.com

CHAPTER FIVE

Stop The Hype & Hard Closes

Sell Even More With
INDIRECT PERSUASION™

Shaune Clarke
Copywriter, Coach & Speaker

Shaune Clarke is... A Canadian talk show host turned marketing consultant and advertising copywriter. Years as a talk show host have given Shaune a unique appreciation for human nature and what moves people to respond. He uses his interviewing skills to uncover the hidden emotions that trigger prospects to buy.

Shaune writes and teaches No-Hype Ad Copy. He says...

"I prefer to use the power of connection, empathy and Indirect PersuasionTM to sell. Rather than creating resistance and 'closing' you can respectfully, yet powerfully, guide the prospect to a buying decision."

Write Down Your Three Most Pressing Marketing or Sales Letter Questions.

Call Shaune, and He'll Answer Them For You... No Charge -- Call Toll-Free 1-866-486-4884

Or Email Him at shaune@dynamicresponsemarketing.com

Copywriters interested in advanced coaching should visit http://www.NewCopySecrets.com

My "New Copy Secrets" Newsletter and "Maximum Website Profits" Checklist Are Available For FREE at... http://www.DynamicResponseMarketing.com

Dynamic Response Marketing
Halifax, Nova Scotia • 1-866-486-4884 • www.ShauneClarke.com

Shaune Clarke

Stop The Hype And Hard Closes
Sell Even More With...
INDIRECT PERSUASION™

Here's How A Canadian Talk-Show Host Turned Marketing Consultant Uses "Indirect Persuasion" To Influence Today's Hyper-Sensitive, Hyper-Resistant Prospects.

It's no secret... sales resistance is at an all-time high. We are constantly bombarded with ads and offers. Benefit-rich marketing messages no longer hold attention as they once did.

Prospects Have Become Numb and Indifferent to Big Promise Marketing.

Today's buyer is beyond skeptical -- he's cynical.

How Do We Persuade Today's Skeptical, More Resistant Prospects?

It's simple... we have to stop hammering them with benefits and trying to "close" the sale. Instead, we must gently lower resistance and guide our prospects to buy. We need to be more respectful. The best way to do this is through "Indirect Persuasion."

What is Indirect Persuasion?

Why does it work so well?
How can you use it?
I'll explain in a moment.
First, it's important to say...

This is NOT Disposable Information.
This is NOT Something You Will Forget Next Week.

I'm going to show you specific examples of Indirect Persuasion and explain why it's so effective. I train up-and-coming copywriters and marketing consultants. Because my goal is to embed this technique into your thought process, I have included a powerful exercise from my coaching program.

At the end of this chapter, you will not only understand Indirect Persuasion, you will know how to use it in your own marketing material.

It's important to remember that your prospect does want to buy. Quite frankly, he's afraid. Afraid of being tricked -- afraid of being taken…again! You must win his trust. How? Don't make him feel pushed to buy. Connect with him. Let him feel your authenticity.

That's the Beauty of Indirect Persuasion™
It Allows You to Pull the Buyer in Subconsciously.
It Works Silently, Beneath the Surface.

He discovers things that move him to buy…on his own. He feels empowered by this "discovery" which creates a strong motivation to buy. Why? Because it was his idea. He doesn't feel pushed into it.

Let everyone else struggle with worn-out marketing methods. Let your competition complain about their 60-hour work weeks. Indirect Persuasion is not over-used. It can't be detected. It is your ticket to increased sales, profitability and more free time.

Here's How To Use Indirect Persuasion™ To
Trigger Specific Conclusions in the Mind of Your Prospect…
Conclusions That Spark the Buying Impulse

In one way or another, it's all about inferring what you want to say. Don't say it directly and don't explain it afterwards. This is a big point. Explaining it afterwards makes them feel told. It completely removes the discovery aspect of it. Discovering it (on their own) really is the power of Indirect Persuasion.

Just make sure there is a close correlation between the point you're making and the impression you want to make. Your prospect's desire and imagination will take care of the rest.

Let's look at an example from a sales letter I wrote for Dr. Tina Maltz, a Naturopathic Physician whose specialty is fertility. This is just one form of Indirect Persuasion. I'll be covering several but wanted to give you a quick sample.

See page 10 for exclusive reader-only FREE offers!

Here it is...

"First let me quickly tell you about my struggle to become pregnant. It's still difficult for me to 'go there', but here goes..."

In the first sentence, Dr. Tina tells us directly that she has had a hard time becoming pregnant. This will connect with the target market. The second sentence appears to be a simple transition sentence, but it's much more than that.

The way it's stated, *"It's still difficult for me to 'go there', but here goes..."*

Read it again -- Especially the words "go there" allow the reader to indirectly feel Dr. Tina's pain. It's inferred. When she says it this way, it's almost like she's talking in "code" to the reader...

What I mean is, someone who's "been there" knows what she means without her having to explain. Someone else wouldn't. It's like talking in shorthand, knowing the person you are talking to will understand automatically.

That's What Makes It So Powerful.
"Indirect Persuasion" Allows the Prospect to
Draw His or Her Own Positive Expectation

For years, I've worked with and refined several different forms of Indirect Persuasion. Their principles do overlap. Trying to understand them all can be overwhelming. Rather than go through all of them I've decided to give you my top four. Using even one will increase your bottom line. Knowing and understanding all four will surely put you ahead of your competition.

Here Are The Four Most Effective Forms of Indirect Persuasion:

- **Real-Life Tidbit** - Use your real life to make a big impact

- **In Passing** - Undetectable to your prospect

- **The Story** - Holds the reader in the buying trance

- **Not Statements** - "Silent," yet dynamic

I've explained them in order. Real-Life Tidbit will be first - In Passing is second - The Story is third and Not Statements is last.

Let's get right to it...

Here's How To Use a "Real-Life Tidbit" to Really Show Them!

You don't want to climb up on a soapbox and shout, "Look at

me!" Instead, show them by sharing a Real-Life Tidbit that has already happened. A Real-Life Tidbit could be a feature of you in a magazine, a document of proof like a sales report or clinical study. My favourite, because it's not overused is showing an actual email you were sent.

Let's look at an example from my own website. (www.DynamicResponseMarketing.com)

Once you get to the site if you scroll down almost to the bottom you'll see an actual email that I sent to a client. There is a story to it but it's the addition of the actual email that makes it a Real-Life Tidbit.

In the email, to offer proof of the effectiveness of what I do, I am showing how something ordinary can be said much better. I began the section by saying...

"Here's a screen shot of an email I sent to Barry T. Noble, the President of BTN Sales Inc. I wrote copy for the PowerPoint presentation he uses to sell international dealerships for an interesting device called Enhance Your Self-Exam."

At the end of the email I explain...

"Number 3 is more personal isn't it? I even took out the word amazing, as it 'felt' better without it. Also, see in number 2, how 'worth the price' was changed in number 3 to 'worth having.' See how it becomes less salesy?"

By putting the actual email right on the site, I increase believability. The email itself gives a "before and after" example of how I would change the sales copy. Not directly, in a more subtle way, this lets my prospect "discover" how I don't use hype -- a big selling point to my target audience -- without specifically saying that.

It's easy to create powerful Real-Life tidbits:

1) Think of tangible elements that can show positive aspects of your business. Documents, reports, or as I've shown, an email.

2) Simply create an image of the piece either by taking a digital photo of it or in the case of an email take a screenshot. (Any good designer can do this.)

The Power of Saying Things... "In Passing"

When you introduce selling points, In Passing, they don't register as part of the sales pitch. They are indirect enough to fly under the radar. It's a simple way to introduce your prospect to powerful parts of your sales message without pushing them.

Earlier, I mentioned writing sales copy for Dr. Tina Maltz. By mentioning, Dr. Tina -- In Passing --there is an assumed credibility. Without knowing it, your belief in the potential of what I offer increased. Your respect for me went up, and it happened without any resistance on your part. You were unaware it was even happening.

To further show the point here's an example of In Passing, from the sales letter I wrote for Dr. Tina:

Every day I hear 'Thank you' from at least one very pregnant and expecting Mother. It is the joy of my life, a purpose I must fulfill.

Dr. Tina makes this, In Passing comment:

"Every day I hear 'Thank you' from at least one very pregnant and expecting Mother"

Read it again, she doesn't directly say, "You will get pregnant"… she doesn't have to! The reasonable conclusion is, "Dr. Tina helps women like me to become mothers. I need her to help me too."

Emotion is what moves our prospects to buy. This sentence helps create the feeling we know our prospect is longing for. By helping her "feel" the joy of motherhood she unconsciously thinks, "I want Dr. Tina to help me too."

Since it's indirect, there's no resistance and even more feeling associated with it.

To create this effect on your own...

1. Determine a feeling you want your prospect to feel before buying your product or service. This is usually the feeling they will have once they experience the benefit of your product or service.

2. Write out a statement that shows this feeling.

3. Now, write out an In Passing comment that eludes to this feeling.

As an example, lets say that the feeling you wanted to convey was safety.

- The statement could be something like… I don't worry anymore.

- The comment you might include in your sales copy could be…

The tension lifted. My husband even commented on how much calmer I was.

See how the feeling we want the prospect to have is generated by this simple In Passing comment?

You'll see a big difference in how your prospects respond when you begin to consciously use In Passing. Next up is how to use The Story.

Think of an Important Piece of Your Sales Message and Ask Yourself... What Story Can I Tell to Bring Out This Essential Point?

Everyone loves a good story. Done well it's very effective. It's my favourite Indirect Persuasion technique.

A story is simply the accounting of something that has happened. It could be an emergency situation, a special event or just a conversation you had. Here's an example from a letter I wrote for a successful network marketing company.

In this piece of their sales letter, the distributor is sharing a conversation he had with the company's receptionist. It's not merely said in passing, it's said in the context of a story.

By including her comment about "new people," this story indirectly shows that new distributors are joining. Here it is...

"Trish, at XYZ Company, suggested I check out the new Business Training Series. She said, "It's so good to hear that raw enthusiasm in people's voice again. The new Business Training Series has really got people going. New distributors seem to respond particularly well."

Growth is a big indicator of opportunity to this target audience. Instead of saying, "1400 new distributors have joined in the last 3 weeks," we inferred that the company was growing -- in the context of a story -- and let the reader "fill in the blanks."

To utilize this form of Indirect Persuasion:

1) Think of stories that reveal a positive aspect of your product or service.

2) To have maximum power, the story should be stated quickly and with short sentences. Write out a critical piece of the story in a few short sentences.

3) Introduce this story by focusing on a different aspect of the conversation, rather than the actual point you want to make. **That's what makes it undetectable.**

4) Trust that the reader will "discover" the extra bit of information on his own. Don't explain it.

Another way to discreetly persuade your prospects is to tell them what your product is not.

"Not Statements" Can Quickly Separate You From The Competition... Here's a real-life example I recently used...

"It's NOT a disinfectant. It's a Sanitizer!"

In this Not Statement, the reader is told directly that there is a difference between a sanitizer and a disinfectant. More importantly, it indirectly suggests that the sanitizer is a superior product.

To discover ways you can use Not Statements, simply make a list of what your product does well and then reverse it to say what it's not.

Here are a few suggestions to get you started.

My product...
- Is not _____ (Something your competition is.)
- Does not contain_____ (What your competition uses.)
- Will not _____ (Something your competition does.)

"Not Statements" are also a convincing way to drive a point home. They are especially effective in counteracting an objection from your prospect.

Let's say you are making an offer but you know that your prospect has been disappointed by similar offers. By using a Not Statement, you can gently assure them that your offer is a valuable one.

Here's an example:

I asked the company, "Want people to get really excited? Give them an unreal deal. And give them that deal on a new hot product, not on something old and tired." They listened and delivered!

I felt the reader's reaction to a simple price cut would be "So what?" They might assume the offer was for some out-of-date product. (It had happened previously.) I wanted them to know that they would get something new and exciting... by saying what it's not.

Here's How Layering Direct and Indirect Statements Can Strengthen Your Point Even More

As he listens to your sales message, your prospect is deciding whether or not he believes the claims you are making. Even though these claims are backed up with proof, he will still have underlying doubts. The effective use of Indirect Persuasion will chip away at his lingering resistance.

Let's use this piece of sales copy as an example.

"At a recent seminar, I spoke with three very excited women -- Theresa, Anne and Barbara. They couldn't wait to share their breakthroughs with me. This is what Barbara had to say..."

We only included one woman's testimonial, (Barbara's) but we described the excitement of all three women. Instead of piling on all three testimonials, one after the other, we used Indirect Persuasion to subtly reinforce our one piece of proof.

It's true...

Embedding even one form of Indirect Persuasion into your sales message can have a huge impact on your success.

Let's start generating Indirect Persuasion ideas for your product or service.

Step 1) Make a list of the conclusions you need your prospects to come to before they will buy.

Step 2) Ask yourself...

- What events, thoughts or people can be closely associated with these conclusions?

- How can I get these ideas across without saying them directly?

3) Follow the exercises outlined throughout the chapter.

To Better Understand the Power of Indirect Persuasion™
Here's the Exercise From My Copywriting Coaching Program.

Slowly read through my sales copy at
http://www.DynamicResponseMarketing.com

As you are reading, note when I say something that has a positive impression on you.

Ask yourself...

1) Why did he pick those words or phrases?

2) What was the event or story that influenced me?

3) What was said in passing?

4) What else helped me to come to these positive conclusions?

Each time you work through this simple exercise, you'll discover more and more ways you can use Indirect Persuasion to reach your prospect.

Closing thoughts, you should consider...

Now more than ever, your prospect is making his purchases based on emotion, trust and gut instinct. Hype no longer works. Hammering prospects with benefits is not enough. You must connect with him on a deeper, more personal level.

Indirect Persuasion lets you slip past conscious awareness and evoke positive emotions. **Your prospects will buy in a manner that feels good to them.**

Put it to work and you will see a dramatic response to your marketing efforts.

See page 10 for exclusive reader-only FREE offers!

FREE!
Continue Your Learning And
Business-Building Online:
www.MDMSbonus.com

CHAPTER SIX

Prove It!

How to Harness the Power of
Testimonials to Increase Sales

Eileen Coale
Copywriter & Consultant

Eileen Coale is an award-winning copywriter, marketing consultant and speaker who works with clients all over the country. Her work includes both online and traditional print media. She specializes in web copy and direct response sales letters, and her clients span a wide variety of industries. She has written for the financial industry, for the traditional and alternative health care fields, and for B2B and B2C companies. Her clients also include coaches, consultants, sales professionals, information marketers, and consumer service providers. Eileen's business has been profiled in a number of publications and she has appeared as a guest on radio shows.

What can you say about someone who delivers on time, on budget and produces killer ad copy that produces a 30% jump in sales? Except, thank you, thank you, thank you. Eileen Coale is an amazing copywriter. I am grateful to her every time I hear the cash register ring!

> Adam Hewison, President
> INO.com, Inc.

You rock! Agents are very excited about the new service I'm offering, and I'm off to a great start - the sales letter you wrote got a 22% response rate! You said it so much better than I could have, and yet it still sounded like me.

> Celia Siegel
> Celia Siegel Management

Coale Communications
Annapolis, MD • 1-888-893-0821 • www.coalecommunications.com

Eileen Coale

Prove It!

How to Harness the Power of Testimonials to Increase Sales

If you're not harnessing the power of testimonials to promote your business, you're missing out on one of the most effective ways to build credibility and interest in your product or service. You're also missing out on increased sales. Every situation is different, but business owners who test sales materials with and without testimonials report that using them translates into significantly more sales.

Testimonials are simply positive comments from a customer about your product or service. Why are they so effective? Because the person who provides the testimonial has nothing to gain by doing it. His praise is seen as objective. Testimonials reassure prospects that you live up to your promises. They overcome skepticism. Testimonials suggest that if someone else gets such great results, the prospect can too.

The riskier the proposition for the prospect, the more important testimonials become. A $3000 conference is a financially riskier proposition than a $20 book. What if the prospect shells out all that money and doesn't learn a thing at the conference? Perhaps a business is asking the prospect to put his health or emotions at risk. How does he know the chiropractor will help rather than hurt his back? How does he know the coach won't secretly think he's a loser? The more testimonials the chiropractor and the coach can provide from satisfied clients, the less vulnerable the prospect feels.

WHERE AND HOW TO USE TESTIMONIALS

Use testimonials liberally in all your marketing materials. Include them in your brochure, on your web site, on the back of your business card, in your direct mail package, in print advertising, and as voice-overs in radio spots. Frame them and hang them on the wall in your reception area, or place them all in a binder on the coffee table.

Don't just sprinkle them randomly, however. Testimonials are most effective when they're precisely placed to support a sales point. For every claim you make, back it up with at least one testimonial. Here's one that supports a garage builder's claim about the quality of construction.

> "I'm impressed with the quality of the materials and the squareness of the construction. The components of the over-head door are top notch."

Testimonials should be specific. This testimonial is for a company that provides commercial laser tag equipment for recreational facilities. Notice all the details that give this testimonial punch.

> "I am impressed with the new arena that you recently installed in my center. It looks great under the black lights and the kids love the new look. The heavy-duty plastic that makes up the columns is super sturdy. It's almost over kill. I have found that the fact there are no sharp corners helps as well."

Another kind of specific testimonial is one that quantifies the results. The following two testimonials do a beautiful job of this. The product is an ebook about writing better Yellow Pages ads.

> "We were just awarded a $25,000 job; a direct result of the client calling us based on our yellow pages ad. He indicated that our ad caught his eye! Thanks!"

> "Thanks for all your help on the ad. It has been working very well. The response to the ad has almost tripled since it has gone out. I recommended you to some other dentist friends of mine (in different regions of course)."

See page 10 for exclusive reader-only FREE offers!

Testimonials can act as mini case studies. Use them to demonstrate how your company solved a particular problem, as in this example:

"I want you to know that I was very pleased with my move from Merrick, NY, to Allentown, Pa. You could not have done a better job. Your crew even saved a $5,000 custom-made sofa that would not fit through the door in our new home. Your crew hoisted it through a small patio and into the living room. What a relief!"

Here's another mini-case study testimonial. While the conventional wisdom would say it's too long, it's not - because it effectively demonstrates how a problem was solved. It also quantifies the results.

"We purchased an [machine name] stretch wrap machine from [company name] about three years ago, and it made a significant improvement in our whole shipping operation. We had previously used tape to wrap pallets, and we had an unacceptable percentage of shipments arrive at their destinations in poor shape. Now, virtually 100% of our shipments arrive in excellent condition. In addition, we are saving money on manual labor and the secure, tightly-bound stretch wrap allows us to stack more product on each pallet, so we have realized a savings in shipping costs as well."

Another technique in using testimonials is to make them comparative. This type of testimonial favorably compares your product or service with an unsatisfactory alternative. Sometimes, the customer will even name the inferior product or company, in essence doing your dirty work for you.

"We switched over to [commercial laser tag system] after 4 1/2 years of using another system, and it was the best decision of the year for us. We can now run several teams at once,   individual play, or a combination of teams and individual play."

"Before [company name], we used another lab, but it took a long time to get results and we had to talk to eight different people to get an answer on anything. [Company name] is very service oriented and when we call people are right there to help."

For every possible objection, spoken or unspoken, place a testimonial near the copy that addresses that objection. Here's one from a company that sells used golf balls.

"I won a bet. I put a new ball down & one of yours. Out of three golfers, no one knew the difference!!!!!!!!!!!!! Thanks."

The unspoken objection here is that used golf balls will look beat up and dirty. Note that I would probably have edited out all the exclamation points.

MORE IS BETTER

The sheer number of testimonials in and of itself is extremely effective. Prospects are unlikely to stop and read every one, but if your business can show that it has literally hundreds of testimonials, the weight of the evidence makes a powerful statement.

My husband and I met in the mid-1980's through a dating service. This was in the days before the internet, and clients had to go into the office to make their selections. Clients were asked to fill out short feedback forms (about a quarter of a page) after each date. The walls of the dating service office were plastered from floor to ceiling with yellow feedback forms, all of them with positive comments. Sitting in the reception room before meeting with the rep, surrounded by page after page of glowing feedback, clients couldn't help but feel optimistic about their future.

To make an even greater impact with your testimonials, involve pictures or audio. In my children's orthodontist's office, there's a before and after picture of every patient's face. The after pictures, of course, feature perfect smiles. I've seen car dealers who have a photograph of every customer they've ever sold to. The customers are always standing, beaming, in front of their new vehicle. In the waiting rooms of obstetricians, I've seen bulletin boards covered with snapshots of precious newborn babies. And we've all see before and after photos for fitness weight and loss ads.

On your website, you can use streaming video or audio and have your satisfied client record their testimonial personally. Marketers are reporting that use of video and audio testimonials on websites is significantly boosting response these days. Master copywriter Clayton Makepeace reported in a recent tele-seminar that streaming audio and video are more than quadrupling response rates for some companies.

See page 10 for exclusive reader-only FREE offers!

SIGNED TESTIMONIALS MEAN
MAXIMUM CREDIBILITY

Credibility is crucial in testimonials. That's why they should always be signed with both first and last names. Let's face it, testimonials signed with just initials - "M.S., Atlanta, Georgia" - make us suspect that it's a made-up person. This can be a tricky issue. Some people are reluctant to have their full names used publicly, especially on the internet. Some companies won't allow their employees to put their names to testimonials for business products. Here are some general guidelines to help give your testimonials maximum credibility.

For consumer products and services, the ideal testimonial contains the customer's first and last name, as well as their city and state. If the customer is reluctant to have both first and last name used, try to negotiate a first initial and last name - e.g., "M. Sanders." It carries more credibility than a first name and last initial, such as "Mark S."

Other identifying information can help to build even more credibility. It can also shore up a testimonial without a last name attached to it. Several years ago, I wrote promotional materials for a personal fitness coach who specialized in working with women 40 and older. Pleased with their results, the clients were all enthusiastic about providing testimonials. But because women are usually sensitive about fitness and weight issues, it came as no surprise that none of them wanted their last names used. Instead, we used their first name, last initial, and their age. The age made a connection with the prospects, who figured if a 72-year old woman could get fit, so could they.

Supplemental identifying information in the signature of the testimonial also makes it easier for prospects to relate to the product. It helps to create a backstory. For instance, I saw a testimonial recently for a pet product that was signed both by the customer and the dog. Here are some examples of how you might use extra information in the signature (assuming it's factual):

- For a product that whitens teeth, include "smoker for 23 years"

- For a carpet stain removal product, "mother of three boys"

- For a glucosamine chondroitin supplement, "53 year old tile-installer"

Customers don't usually think to add this type of information to their testimonials when they write them. If you design a system for getting testimonials (more about that shortly), this is something you'll want to take into consideration.

For business-to-business testimonials, first and last names are just the starting point. You should also use the job title and company of the person who signs the testimonial whenever possible. Some companies won't permit this - "Marshall Lynch, Vice President, First National Bank" - but will permit a descriptive phrase to be used instead, like this: "M. Lynch, senior executive, financial institution."

DON'T WAIT FOR THEM
TO COME TO YOU

If you wait for testimonials to come to you, you may be waiting a long time. It happens, but not as often as you'd like. That's why having a system in place to get testimonials is essential. Build transaction follow-up into your customer relationship management processes so that you have a systematic, ongoing way of getting testimonials.

When you do receive an unsolicited testimonial, contact the customer and ask permission to use it with their full name (and any other information you need, such as their city or business name). Get permission in writing or via email. Send the individual a release form in the mail with a pre-addressed stamped envelope to encourage a reply.

You can also get permission via email. Or you can fax a release form and request a reply by return fax. I prefer email and fax, because it keeps the momentum going. If you send something in the mail, it's too easy for it to get stuck in a pile or for the customer to have second thoughts.

Most of the time, you'll need to be proactive about asking for testimonials. Shortly after you've delivered a product or completed a service, there's often a "honeymoon period." For a time, you're the customer's new best friend. Often, it's linked to a breakthrough solution or rapid progress.

Seize the moment, and ask for a testimonial. Make it easy for the customer. If you're on the phone with him, ask if you can transcribe down his comments immediately. Email or fax them over for his immediate approval.

See page 10 for exclusive reader-only FREE offers!

Design a telephone or mail program specifically designed to get customer feedback shortly after a transaction concludes. One way to do this is to create a mailing program or email auto-responder program with a customer satisfaction survey. The survey should go out shortly after the transaction is over. If it takes a few weeks or months for the customer to implement the solution and start seeing results, time your request appropriately.

You can also interview your long-time customers, or have a third party do it. Assign the job to someone from your customer service department, or to an outside marketing consultant or copywriter. The advantage to having a third party do it is that it usually makes the customer more comfortable.

Customer interviews are also an opportunity to ask for feedback on how you can improve services. The customer is usually more comfortable giving constructive feedback to a third party than they are directly to you. Interviews provide an opportunity to dig deeper and explore the customer's comments further. You can ask clarifying questions and glean the specifics you're looking for.

FINAL DO'S AND DON'TS

There are ethical and legal issues to consider when using testimonials. For starters, they must be based on actual use of the product or service. They cannot be made up. In some industries, you're required to keep records on file with full contact information, dates, and other pertinent information.

Resist the temptation to rewrite them to make them sound better. Authenticity makes a stronger connection with the customer than lyrical language. Edit them if necessary, or insert punctuation to make them clear, but be sure it doesn't change the meaning or mislead the reader.

Finally, keep your testimonials up to date. No matter how perfect a testimonial may be, you should restock your testimonial library regularly. All businesses change over time, and you want testimonials to speak to the current aspects of your business.

TESTIMONIAL CHECKUP:
ARE YOUR TESTIMONIALS DOING THE JOB?

☐ You have more than one or two testimonials on your website.

☐ You have more than half a dozen testimonials to use on all your marketing materials.

☐ You have a system in place for gathering testimonials.

☐ You have updated your testimonials with new ones in the past 18 months.

☐ The testimonials you have mention quantifiable results or specific benefits.

☐ Each testimonial carries a credible attribution.

☐ You keep accurate records and have permission from each person who gave you a testimonial.

If you left any of these statements "unchecked," go to www.proofpackage.com immediately for in-depth assistance with your testimonial program.

FREE!
**Continue Your Learning And
Business-Building Online:
www.MDMSbonus.com**

CHAPTER SEVEN

Baby Got Back-End!

How To Reclaim 70% to 90% of Your Lost Profits by Harnessing the Power of Repeat Sales

Lee & Robin Collins

*Speakers, Authors &
Business Consultants*

Lee and Robin spent nearly 10 years in the United States Air Force where they first met while serving in Korea; marking the beginning of their incredibly successful partnership.

After consulting with dozens of global companies over the years, in early 2001, they shifted their business direction to focus on small to medium size business owners. This allowed them to realize their dream of a more personalized venue to teach and assist a more fledgling community.

This also allowed them to grow their business to astounding heights. A notable highlight would be their first 6-digit month in 2002 achieved by following their unique marketing strategies which would later be compiled into their flagship product and provided to customers as a 4-week workshop and eCourse called "One Page Money Makers™."

Lee and Robin's guidance has helped thousands of customers grow and succeed in their own businesses and to realize their financial and personal ambitions and has been instrumental in selling hundreds of thousands of dollars worth of products for a wide range of clients in unrelated markets.

Through their line of products and successful public speaking engagements, Lee and Robin strive to show everyone they can achieve whatever they dream simply by having and following a proven plan of action.

SOCO Solutions
Fenton, MI • 810-597-7381 • www.socosolutions.com

Lee & Robin Collins

Baby Got Back-End!

How To Reclaim 70% to 90% of Your Lost Profits by Harnessing the Power of Repeat Sales

OK, you have spent all this time, money, energy and desire getting your business off the ground. You have your business and products… you have decided on and put into action your marketing strategy.

You've sweated (and maybe even cried a little) bringing it all together. And then it happened…

Your fresh, new customers start to show up. Rock On!

Now you need to ask yourself, is this all there is?

I believe you already know that answer… and that's...

"ABSOLUTELY NOT!"

Think about it this way…

If you're going to spend the remainder of your business life focused on making only one sale per customer, you're going to be continually working and trying to overcome the hardest thing in business - making that first sale.

In fact, studies have shown that it's an estimated 8-11 times more difficult to make the first sale than it is to make subsequent sales to the same customer!

That means after the first sale your customer is much more likely to buy from you again - assuming of course you provided a good product or service.

If you have failed to work out in advance what you will sell them next or something additional you can up sell them during the initial sales transaction - you are literally leaving money on the table.

Back-end sales is simply providing the next logical solution to your customer's next logical need.

It's your **DUTY** to identify that next logical need, to create the solution for that need and continually sell and sell again to fill it.

Now we're NOT talking about the hard-core, in your face sales tactics. We're talking about allowing the customer to make a 2nd or 3rd buying decision based on their satisfaction with their first experience with you.

As a business owner, you need to realize early on that your customers actually need to be led from one purchase to the next.

This is true not only in business but also in many aspects of our lives.

There are times when we want someone to tell us what to do so we don't have to make that decision ourselves.

Have you ever heard a conversation that goes something like this:

Person 1: "Hey, what do you want to do?"

Person 2: "I don't care, what do you want to do?"

Person 1: "I don't care, I'll do whatever you want to do."

Person 2: "Well, it doesn't matter to me."

Then when one person actually makes a decision, the other inevitably says "no."

And so it goes! You've probably even had this conversation yourself!

The point is that we as consumers need you to tell us what we need next.

This leads us to the topic at hand… Back-End Sales.

After I buy from you the first time - what happens next?

If I could sum up the process of creating back-end sales in four simple steps, they would be:

1. Making the Initial Sale

To keep this chapter focused on back-end sales, we will assume that you have marketed correctly to get that initial sale.

This sale is simply the first "exchange" of goods or services between you and your customer.

2. Add-on Products

Your first question may be, "What the heck are add-on products?"

For an easy example, think of your favorite fast food restaurant.

You just ordered your cheeseburger with ketchup and a medium soda. What are always the next words out of the cashier's mouth..."Would you like fries with that?"

That's an add-on. A back-end.

This up-sell generates millions of dollars for these fast food chains each year.

So, that's one strategy.

Your task is to figure out what you can offer at the time of your product sale as an add-on and watch your profits climb.

One tip though, be sure the add-on makes sense.

Think about it... you wouldn't sell a print cartridge add-on with your cheeseburger order, right? Maybe you would, if you're weird.

3. Customer Follow Up

Building a continued relationship with your customers is a critical piece of the puzzle. This point is so important that it has filled dozens of books all on its own.

But just to hit on this a little to show you how it ties into the importance of our back-end sales process ...

Like we mentioned above, a person who has already purchased from you is much more likely to buy from you again. So part of your marketing should absolutely include some type of customer follow up.

During this follow up, you will provide your customer with information on other products related in some way to the items they have already purchased.

This WILL lead to additional sales. Plain and simple.

If you're NOT following up - you're losing money every day!

4. Discounts and Bonuses

Providing a discount coupon that a customer can use on their next purchase is incredible incentive for the customer to buy from you again.

This does two things...

1. It shows the customer that you have additional products

2. The customer will feel appreciated and this helps build a trust with you.

Picture yourself as a consumer who has just had the oil in your car changed.

You pay for the service and the technician slips you a discount coupon for your next visit. Where will you go for your next service? The same place, of course!

And what about bonuses?

Providing your customer with an unexpected bonus can hugely increase your back-end sales. The trick is to make sure that you tie the bonus back to another one of your products and that it is related to the initial purchase.

For example, you buy a dozen glazed donuts from your local bakery. The bakery throws in a bonus donut. But it isn't a glazed donut - it is their new custard filled, chocolate covered pastry.

Sure, you're happy because they just gave you a free donut.

But think how happy the baker is when the sales of this new pastry soar by providing it as a bonus in each order.

I believe you're starting to get the idea, but usually at this point is where we're told by some of our clients...

BUT I DON'T HAVE A BACK-END PRODUCT

You might say, "But I don't have any product or service to sell as an up-sell."

The short response is always, yes you do. You just haven't realized it.

*(And if I must entertain that you DON'T have one,
then I'll say to you it's time to develop one. If you don't,
you are simply leaving money on the table and
letting your customers down.)*

OK, let's do a little brainstorming...

Get a piece of paper and a pen.

Here are 3 great tips that will help you develop your back-end product or service:

1. Can you break up your product into smaller offerings?

You don't necessarily want to sell your whole product all at once.

Unless you have very little competition, you may benefit greater by breaking your product up into smaller offerings.

This will allow you to offer your product to the same customer on a recurring and frequent basis, growing that customer relationship that we know will lead to further sales.

Besides, some customers may be hesitant to make the commitment of your full product.

See page 10 for exclusive reader-only FREE offers!

You may want to give them an opportunity to give you a test drive with a smaller, less expensive portion of your product. We will get into this more a little later.

2. Do you provide a product? What related service could you offer?

Everyone is an expert at something. You are likely an expert on the product or product area you are currently selling.

You could offer your opinion, guidance and inside information as a consultant or teacher.

For example, you own a wild bird supply retail store. You obviously know more about wild birds than most of your customers.

Why not offer a weekly class on the different species in the area, what the benefits of some species have over others and how to attract them to your back yard?

Think about what product you are offering and what questions your customer typically asks. There is your backend product -it's you!

Or maybe you sell audio equipment. For fun, let's say high-end equipment.

Joe Customer comes into the store and wants to buy a new receiver, but really isn't familiar with the terminology or specifications.

Along with your personal service, you sell him a "How To Guide for High End Audio". You could also recommend other products in the guide to help him discover what to look for in speakers, speaker wires, connecting cables, and so on.

Maybe you have a "High End Audio Workshop" every Thursday at 7pm to help people make better decisions about their home theater purchase.

Where do you think Joe is going to go next time he has something he wants to buy?

Now let's flip it around ...

3. Do you provide a service? What related products could you offer?

As an example, we recently had our "overgrown field of a front yard" converted into a beautifully landscaped scene of tranquility. (OK, maybe a little over board there...)

The landscaping company owner, Bill, works with his crew on each job.

We spoke with Bill frequently while the crew was cooling off in the shade.

During one discussion, we discovered that his company had access to reduced cost supplies that they use in providing their service.

I immediately chimed in..."Do you resell these products?"

It was at this point that he had a realization. I could see the light bulb as he said, "No, I never thought of that but you can bet that I will now."

See, Bill was missing a huge opportunity by not providing these supplies to others. He already had an interested contact in the homeowner and now he realized a way to use his supply as a back-end product line for projects the homeowners wanted to do themselves.

Are you starting to get the picture?

TIME FOR THE SUPER SECRET TIP

Now, all of the back-end sales techniques we have talked about DO work and will have you increasing your profits almost immediately.

However, I do not want you to get the wrong idea that you even have to make the first sale before you can start working the back-end.

Huh?

Let me say that again...

You do not have to make a single initial sale to leverage the profit-pulling machine of back-end sales!

In many cases, you can make huge profits simply by giving your product away.

Picture this example:

You are walking through the grocery store.

Tummy growling because you broke the cardinal rule and went grocery shopping on an empty stomach.

You spot a free sample tray of chocolate chip cookies across the aisle.

Little bite-size nuggets of crispy, chocolaty goodness arranged neatly on a platter with toothpicks for you to indulge yourself in one delicious bite.

Do you grab one of those delicious, free cookies? You bet you do!

And after enjoying every bite of that soft, chewy chocolaty cookie (or two) do you grab a box of those very same cookies from the display stand set up conveniently next to the sample tray?

Again - you know you do! You just took the bait of a free sample and your need was fulfilled by the back-end product.

Still don't believe it works?

See page 10 for exclusive reader-only FREE offers!

Fact: The Mrs. Fields' EMPIRE was built by giving away free samples of cookies in shopping malls.

It can and does work. Believe it!

BUT I DON'T SELL COOKIES - HOW CAN I USE THIS TECHNIQUE?

We will get to that in a minute, but first let's touch on why this works.

It works because consumers often times don't want to jump in and commit to a purchase. Put more scientifically it's called "the Law of Reciprocity".

They may want to dip their "big toe" in the water and sample the product in a relatively risk-free and painless way. After all, getting your big toe cold will not lead to freezing to death.

It's an easy risk to take while deciding whether or not to jump all the way in.

Once they've sampled your "cookie" they feel more compelled to "give back" by giving you their business.

Granted, your marketing will bring in some customers who will pick up that pack of cookies without needing to be tempted by a sample. But you aren't doing your job as a business owner if you don't try to capture those unconvinced customers.

Much money is left on the table ignoring the "non-buying" segment of your customers!

HERE ARE SIX KEY POINTS YOU NEED TO TAKE AWAY FROM THIS CHAPTER:

#1 Your customer's first purchase is not their full purchasing ability. It's just the tip of the iceberg. The real money is in the back-end sales and the "lifetime value" of your customer.

#2 If you don't have a product or service to use as a back-end offer, create one. Do it today.

#3 Your customer may need to be provided with a low or no-risk offer to try you out in a small, non-threatening way. Your customers often need to be led down the path with small commitments happening over a period of time.

#4 Don't forget to up-sell the customer with an add-on at the time of the sale.

#5 Slip the customer a discount or bonus to drive repeat business. Insurance companies are masters at this. So are online businesses like Amazon.com.

#6 Give it away for free to work the back-end. Think about AOL.com when they first started offering the free Internet Service CD's. They took huge losses on the front-end to make millions on the back-end.

STILL STUCK? HERE ARE A FEW QUICK EXAMPLES TO GET YOU THINKING:

- Pest control companies offer a free inspection, and then attempt to up-sell you their service contracts as a back-end. This technique also works for heating and cooling, lawn care, and other service industries.

- Car dealerships usually make little to no money on the vehicle sale, but make huge profits on the extended warranties, floor mats, or rust protection. Some have even partnered with businesses like paint and customization shops, or audio specialists to help personalize the experience.

- Today's insurance companies offer much more than just insurance for your home. They also may offer auto, boat, renter's or personal insurance as well as a variety of other services like banking and investing. Become a customer for just one of these services and you will see a masterful use of the back-end strategy first-hand.

The big point here is this ...

You need to realize that the biggest mistake a business owner can make is believing that once they have made their first sale of a product or service to the customer, that is the end of the process.

Nothing could be further from the truth.

Every sale needs another sale because every need that is satisfied will create still another need. It should be a never-ending process.

Back-end sales and the never-ending cycle of getting the customer to purchase the next item is the most important step in any effective marketing campaign and all truly successful businesses.

See page 10 for exclusive reader-only FREE offers!

FREE!

**Continue Your Learning And
Business-Building Online:
www.MDMSbonus.com**

CHAPTER EIGHT

Results-Driven Radio

7 Keys to Making a Fortune Using Radio Advertising

Ray Edwards

Copywriter & Marketing Strategist

Ray Edwards is a Copywriter and Business Growth Strategist based in Spokane, Washington, USA.

His firm was nominated to Fast Company Magazine's "Fast 50" for 2005.

"My specialty is one thing," Ray says, "and that is to write copy that produces profits."

With over 25 years experience in the radio broadcasting and marketing business, Ray has worked with hundreds of businesses - writing copy, creating promotions, and developing strategies that increase sales and profits.

Ray is known for being able to quickly grasp complex marketing problems and turn those into persuasive copy that motivates customers and prospects to take action.

As a Business Growth Strategist, Ray helps you create a business strategy that increases sales, multiplies profits, and reduces costs. Ray is also a sought-after speaker and published author.

Ray Edwards International, Inc.
Spokane, WA • 1-800-780-4345 • www.RayEdwards.com

<u>Ray Edwards</u>

Results-Driven Radio

7 Keys to Making a Fortune Using Radio Advertising

Radio advertising is an often-overlooked "magic marketing bullet." Done correctly, it can increase your profits like magic. Done wrong, you can burn money at stunning speeds.

This chapter gives you the 7 Keys to doing radio advertising the right way. But first...

THE POWER OF RADIO

Think about the advertising that you actually remember. Can you complete any of these phrases?

- "Plop, plop, fizz, fizz, oh what a…"
- "Two all beef patties, special sauce, lettuce, cheese…"
- "Winston tastes good like a…"

Chances are you know the answers are:

- "…relief it is." Alka Seltzer
- "…pickles onions on a sesame seed bun." McDonald's Big Mac™ recipe jingle
- "…cigarette should." Winston cigarettes

We remember these ads in their entirety because of the distinctive audio that made a powerful impression on our brains.

That's the power of radio advertising done well.

Here are the 7 Keys to Making a Fortune Using Radio Advertising...

KEY 1: USE DIRECT RESPONSE COPY

Most radio ads use ineffective copy - they try to be funny, cute, or clever. Don't use these tactics because they almost never work. Instead, use a direct response ad.

You've heard direct response ads on radio already, especially if you listen to talk radio. These ads often feature only the announcer's voice, with no distracting background music or special effects, and they make a very clear "call to action" (e.g. "call now for free information...").

A good basic template for such an ad looks like this:

1. Attention-grabbing headline

2. Associate the listener to the main benefit of your product or service.

3. Describe the offer in vivid language.

4. Re-associate the listener to the benefit.

5. Make a direct call to action (repeat at least three times).

I recommend the call to action, whenever possible, be either a website address or a phone number.

Once you have convinced the prospect to take one of those two actions, you can place them into your marketing system to make the sale.

To illustrate this process in action, I have included two sample radio ads; one done the "usual" way (ineffective), and one done the correct (direct response) way.

Wrong Way to Do a Radio Ad (the "Usual" Way)

"Craft Master Jewelers is proud to announce our 20th annual Valentine Sale! Come browse the enormous selection of the finest diamond and gold jewelry available anywhere. Come on in to our store at 1313 Mockingbird Lane, and see for yourself as our friendly courteous staff helps you make the right decision about what jewelry to buy. We have tennis bracelets, solitaires, and even custom pieces available. We have over 75 years experience and are eager to serve you. Call us at 555-1212, visit our website at Craft Master Jewelers, or stop by the store at 1313 Mockingbird Lane today."

See page 10 for exclusive reader-only FREE offers!

Here are some of the problems with the ad copy above:

- It uses a lot of cliché language that listeners will tune out: "enormous selection," "friendly courteous staff," and "eager to serve you." This is useless chatter that nobody listens to.

- The ad is not about the listener, it's about the advertiser: "Craft Master Jewelers…proud to announce," "our store," "our staff," "we have," etc.

- Too many options for the listener: tennis bracelets, solitaires, custom pieces, enormous selection.

- Too many conflicting calls to action, none of them clear: the phone number, the web address, the street address. What's the customer/listener supposed to do?

Now let's look at an ad for the same company, done using a different approach...

Right Way to Do a Radio Ad - "Direct Response" Style

"Attention - men who still haven't bought that Valentine's gift. It's not too late to make her glow with love for you. Imagine...a jewelry craftsperson asks you a few simple questions, and then creates the perfect gift of diamonds or gold. All without the frustrating shopping experience, in a minimum of time, and at the price you choose. Enjoy her surprise and delight... call Craft Master Jewelers now at 555-1212.... 555-1212 Don't disappoint her - delight her instead. 555-1212."

What's right about the second ad?

- The focus is entirely where it should be; on the harried, busy, clueless man who hasn't bought his wife or sweetheart a Valentine's gift.

- The headline speaks directly to the intended target - "men who still haven't bought that Valentine's gift."

- The body copy talks about benefits that are important to the men who are most likely to buy jewelry: their concern over budgets, time efficiency, and the fact that they hate shopping. Is that romantic? No. Will it bring the jewelry store customers with money in their wallets, ready to spend? Yes. Because it speaks to the needs of the customer.

- The call to action (the phone number) is direct, simple, and repeated 3 times.

KEY 2: ANY STATION WORKS, IF YOU BUY ENOUGH ADS

While it certainly doesn't hurt to be on top-rated stations, it's not necessary. The top-rated station usually has the most expensive ad rates. You don't have to be on the #1 station -- there's no reason you can't advertise on any of the stations in the Top 10 as rated by the Arbitron Ratings Company.

Over 90% of the available audience listens only to the stations in the Top 10. You don't have to choose between 40 stations in your area. Just look at the Top 10, and pick a station (or stations) that seem to fit the profile of your target customer. For example, if you're selling products meant for Baby Boomers, the Hip-Hop station probably is not the place to advertise.

Beyond these criteria (targeting radio audiences based on their lifestyle), any station will work. All you need to do is pick a station, and run a lot of ads (high "frequency") over an extended period of time. A good minimum ad schedule to consider is:

Monday - Sunday

- 6am - 10am (one ad)
- 10am - 3pm (one ad)
- 3pm - 7pm (one ad)
- 7pm - Mid (one ad)
- Mid - 6am (you should be able to get one ad per hour in this timeslot for peanuts...maybe for nothing!)

KEY 3: MAKE EACH AD CONTAIN ONLY ONE MOST WANTED RESULT

You cannot have an effective radio ad that tries to get multiple actions, or achieve multiple goals. Many radio advertisers will try to do too many things in a single commercial: get a mention in for their street address, their phone number, their website, and their "special of the week."

See page 10 for exclusive reader-only FREE offers!

No consumer will remember any of those things - they'll just tune out your ad.

Yet that's what most radio ads sound like.

You must decide in advance: what is the purpose for your ad? What is the Most Wanted Result you need to get from your ad?

You can ask consumers to visit a website, or to call a phone number, or even to visit your physical store…but if you try and ask for all those results in a single ad, you'll likely get none of them.

There can be only one "Most Wanted Result" for each ad you run.

KEY 4: DON'T LET THE RADIO PEOPLE WRITE YOUR COPY

Here's a dirty little secret of the radio business: over 95% of the ads are written by the salesperson or by a DJ.

Almost no stations employ full-time copywriters.

Do you really want a salesperson or DJ writing your copy? (The answer is, "NO.")

Even if the radio station (or ad agency) has a full-time writer, chances are the writer will be more interested in writing "cute" or "award-winning" copy.

"Award-winning" copy almost never equals "sales-making" copy.

If it's sales and profits that interest you, don't let the radio people write your copy. Write it yourself, or hire a copywriter who is well-versed in writing direct response-style radio copy.

KEY 5: NEVER WORK WITH CHILDREN OR COMEDIANS

For some reason, many radio advertisers feel compelled to try making their commercials "cute" or "funny." It almost never works.

One common mistake: using a cute kid's voice in their ad. The cuter the voice, they think, the more attention people will pay to it. That's true…but that's also the problem.

Using a cute kid voice almost always means the listener will focus only on how cute the voice is…and they will be distracted from listening to the ad's intended message.

An effective radio ad creates a picture in the mind of the listener, and that picture is of the listener enjoying the benefits of your product or service. I call this the "benefit picture."

When a listener is only focused on the cute kid voice in your ad, they don't see themselves benefiting from your product or service, and thus they don't take the action you want them to take.

Using humor in your ads is a bad idea because it's hard to be funny. It's even harder to be funny in a way that creates a benefit picture in the listener's mind.

How many times have you told a friend about some very funny commercial you saw on TV or heard on the radio, only to realize you couldn't remember what product or company the ad was for?

Bottom line: when you leave off the cute and the funny ads, you're going to be left with an ad that might seem boring to your friends and family. But that "boring" ad will be much more likely to bring you the customers, leads, and profits you desire.

KEY 6: BUY EVERYTHING BUT DRIVE TIME

Radio sales people love to sell commercials in what's called "drive-time" (the hours each day most people are driving to and from work, usually 6am - 10am and 3pm - 7pm). They love to sell these commercials because (a) they're easy to sell, and (b) drive-time spots are the most expensive spots on the radio station - so the commissions for the salesperson are bigger.

When your budget is tight - or when you are testing a new commercial to see how effective it is (how much response it gets) - I suggest a different strategy.

Buy spots every hour outside of morning and afternoon drive times (morning drive is the single most expensive advertising real estate on almost every radio station; afternoon drive is next).

That means one spot per hour:

- Midnight - 6am
- 10am-3pm
- 7pm - Midnight

You can normally get these commercials at a great discount.

In fact, ask for the commercials from Midnight - 6am as a "free bonus" for buying the others. Quite often you'll get them free - or at least for dirt cheap rates.

See page 10 for exclusive reader-only FREE offers!

If you have a bit more money, or if you tested your ad and it seems to be working well, try buying one commercial in each drive time, at the same time every day (so the same people hear the same ad day in and day out). If that works, you can expand your buying into other drive time hours.

KEY 7: USE THIS SECRET TACTIC TO IGNITE YOUR AD RESPONSE

The most popular time-slot on most radio stations is the morning show, which is usually on the air Monday-Friday, 6am-10am.

These are the hours during which the station almost always has its biggest audience. Listeners tend to be most loyal to a station's morning personalities and DJs.

If you can get interviewed on the morning show in a favorable light, it can put the rest of your advertising on steroids. If the audience thinks the morning show likes you and your product, it's as if you've been endorsed by the show. This can be an enormous boost for your sales.

You can often make a morning show interview a condition of your advertising contract. One caution: make sure you are not being "forced" on the morning show's host(s).

If the host feels you're being forced on them by the sales department, it can cause resentment. If that's the case, don't do the interview until you're certain you're welcome. Being interviewed in a sarcastic or unfavorable light can be worse than no interview at all.

Win the host(s) over to your cause, make them like you, and you've unlocked the profits vault.

FINAL THOUGHTS: DON'T MAKE THESE MISTAKES IN RADIO ADVERTISING

Common mistakes to avoid when advertising on radio:

- Not having a clear Call to Action.

- Too many ideas or products presented in one commercial.

- Not running the ad frequently enough or over a long enough period of time.

- Poor use of humor.

- Using cute kid voices.

- Using background music, sound effects, and other distractions in the commercial.

- Using cliché phrases that are ignored by listeners: "save like never before," "friendly courteous staff," "conveniently located," "savings throughout the store," "everything must go"…omit useless phrases.

- Trying to cram too much copy into an ad - or not writing enough copy to fill an ad's allotted time. You want just enough copy for the announcer to read the copy at a normal, natural pace. To get the copy exactly the right length: time yourself while reading the copy out loud.

- Using the station's DJs to voice the copy, which makes your ad sound like every other ad on the station (because the same DJs do those ads, too). Pay the extra money to hire a voiceover talent from outside the market to voice your copy. One exception: if you are getting a personal endorsement from the DJ, let them do the ad.

What to Do Now

You now know more than 93% of business owners about the right way to advertise on the radio. Put the power of what you know into action!

Radio can build your business quickly, increasing sales and profits literally overnight.

Put these 7 Keys to work in your radio advertising campaigns and start enjoying increased sales and profits.

See page 10 for exclusive reader-only FREE offers!

FREE!
**Continue Your Learning And
Business-Building Online:
www.MDMSbonus.com**

CHAPTER NINE

Conversational Selling Strategies

How To Get Prospects To Close Themselves

Ed Forteau

Strategic Marketing Coaching,
Sales Advisor & Author

Ed Forteau, known as "The Strategic Marketing Coach," is the president of Win/Win Professional Marketing & Sales Association. Ed has been a marketing and sales advisor to small businesses and professional practices for over 16 years. His innovative techniques have been taught and implemented by hundreds of business owners, both in the U.S. and abroad.

Ed's marketing methods have been written about in Entrepreneur Magazine, City Business, The Business Journal, and countless newspapers. He has also appeared on radio and television. He is a published author, and his marketing and advertising articles have been published in dozens of major professional trade journals, newsletters, magazines, and newspapers.

Ed's Strategic Marketing Coach Selling System™ (SMC Selling System™) has transformed ordinary salespeople into sales superstars. His "Ethical Persuasion" approach to selling takes all the pressure off buyers and sellers, causing buyers to close themselves. And his experience working with business professionals in over 38 different industries has contributed to the selling system being able to work in any business, in any industry.

Discover how you can benefit from Ed's wisdom by visiting his website at www.StrategicMarketingCoach.com. Call him today to obtain limited access to his members' area, and view his 30 minute SMC Selling System™ training video.

Strategic Marketing Coach
Stanton, MI • 1-866-835-9433 • www.StrategicMarketingCoach.com

<u>Ed Forteau</u>

Conversational Selling Strategies
How To Get Prospects To Close Themselves

The function of marketing is to facilitate an effective sales process. In this book, you have discovered many effective ways to use marketing to attract prospects to you. Now that you have these prospects, you need to close the sale and turn them into customers. In this chapter, I will share with you a unique selling system that gets prospects to close themselves.

In many ways, selling is like the game of chess. You make a move, then the prospect makes a move. That process goes back and forth until you get one of three outcomes. A "Yes" - which means the prospect decides to purchase your product or service. A "No" - which means the prospect decides not to purchase your product or service. Or a "Lesson" - which means something else happened.

Your first goal with a prospect should be to get to a point of having an honest conversation. Get the other person to put down their guard, and feel comfortable that they are not going to get taken advantage of by some huckster. You would think this would be simple, but it's not. People have their guards up the minute you engage them. No one will buy from you until they trust you - and trust is not given, it is earned.

You may be shocked to read this, but prospects sometimes lie. I know. I know. But it IS true. Don't blame them; it is just a defense mechanism. It has proven to help them in the past from being taken advantage of. This is why getting to the point of having an honest conversation is so important.

YOU NEED TO BOND WITH YOUR PROSPECT

Studies have shown that as much as 83% of the sale depends upon whether the prospect/customer likes the salesperson. It shouldn't be surprising that Bonding & Rapport are a critical component of getting the sale.

There are three rules to the effective use of Bonding & Rapport:

1. Make the person feel good about himself or herself.
2. Nurture the person by offering them reassurance & support.
3. Focus on their dangers and opportunities (pains, consequences, and goals).

Let's start with making the person feel good about himself or herself. This is all about the prospect feeling OK. People determine their OKness in relations to others. So the key here is to be slightly less OK than the prospect. One way to be slightly less OK than the prospect is to struggle on purpose. Here are a few ways to struggle on purpose:

1. Use phrases that help clarify what the prospect is saying such as, "I don't understand," or "Can you help me with that?" or "What do you mean, exactly?"

2. Even if you know the answer to everything, act like you don't. Tell the prospect that they asked a very good question. Then say that you are not 100% sure of the answer, but you will check for them.

3. Allow the prospect to "know it all" so they can get their OKness needs met. Never play the one-upmanship game with a prospect.

Nurture the person by offering them reassurance and support. As you take a prospect through the selling system, they will most likely experience varying degrees of fear. First, you will be identifying a problem that they have, which is discomforting in itself. Second, they will realize the cost of the problem (both emotionally and financially), and that they will need to invest money and time to solve it. Third, they may have failed in trying to solve this problem in the past, and don't want to fail again. This leads to putting their ego and

See page 10 for exclusive reader-only FREE offers!

esteem at risk. Because of this, the prospect is going to need you to provide a great degree of comfort, encouragement, and reassurance.

Finally, you will want to discuss their pains, consequences, and goals. You are in the business of solving problems. Unless the prospect is an existing customer, the prospect is going to have to change behaviors, if they decide to do business with you. When this happens, the prospect will go through something we call the Pain of Change, and the Consequences of Not Changing.

The Pain of Change involves all of the prospect's feelings and experiences associated with new behavior and doing something different.

Consequences of Not Changing are all of the penalties your prospects incur because they are not doing business with you. This could include financial and emotional penalties.

When you initiate contact, most of your prospects believe that they are doing quite well without you. They also believe that if there are consequences associated with not doing business with you, those consequences are quite acceptable. If either belief is true, you don't have a prospect.

Before you will ever make the sale, you must successfully introduce the concept that there are indeed consequences associated with not doing business with you, because if there are no consequences, there is little or no chance of them buying. If there are consequences, bring them up in the form of a question (that is totally different from talking about "what you do." This is what all salespeople do). When you do this consequences step, you will bring to the surface what your prospect will experience in the absence of a relationship with you (and access to what you do).

In the following example, a luxury car dealer uses questions to differentiate itself from the competition. The advantage this car dealer offers is to pick up your car, and/or provide you with a loaner car while your car is in for scheduled service.

"When you talked to the other car dealer about how they ensure you are not inconvenienced when your car needs to be serviced, what did they tell you?"

The salesperson is relatively certain that the prospect never asked the other car dealer this question. It positions them against their competition, and invites the prospect to inquire about this higher level of service. The salesperson does not come across as pompous. He is perceived as a helpful advisor who is answering their questions. This subtle difference moves you from being perceived as a salesperson to a trusted advisor.

This method of Bonding & Rapport goes beyond the typical small talk that buyers and sellers engage in. It allows you to remain focused on the reasons the two of you are talking in the first place. Most importantly, it gives the prospect the feeling that you understand them…and one of our basic human needs is to be understood.

SALES MANEUVERS THAT CLOSE SALES

Just as in the game of chess, in sales chess we have labels for the different sales maneuvers we use. In the Strategic Marketing Coach Selling System™, there are over 200 different maneuvers at our disposal for moving the prospect through our selling system, and ultimately gaining a yes or no decision.

The three primary maneuvers we use are Crossover Moves, Fade Moves, and Cushion Statements.

Crossover Moves - Answering a question with a question. Crossover Moves play on the social obligation that has been ingrained in us from childhood, in that when someone asks us a question, we are obligated to give them an answer. Crossover Moves disarm the prospect by doing the opposite of what they expect, resulting in less resistance.

Fade Moves - Statements that causes the prospect to convince themselves, while allowing you to stay in a safe position on the pendulum (to be discussed shortly). When you use Fade Moves, you psychologically back up from the prospect to get them to move towards you.

Cushioning Statements - Statements used before a Crossover or Fade Move to soften (or cushion) the move. Short acknowledgements of what your prospects need keeps them comfortable. These cushioning statements keep the Crossover and Fade Moves from sounding like an interrogation.

The moves you are most likely to encounter from a prospect are Fat Words & Phrases, Head Fakes, and Objections.

Fat Words & Phrases - An intellectual response your prospect uses which has no concrete meaning. Examples of Fat Words include (but are not limited to): Maybe, possibly, considering, might, perhaps, thinking about, exploring, looking into, etc.

Head Fakes - Are things that prospects say to hide their true interest (or lack of interest). Head fakes are used by prospects to get free advice from the seller, negotiate better terms, or hide their true intentions.

Objections - Are barriers the prospect brings up that stand in the way of the sale.

Let's look at an example of each of these maneuvers, so you can see how they are used in a selling situation.

Crossover Moves

Crossover Moves consist of two parts: the build-up and the take-away. Here's an example:

"The Strategic Marketing Coach Selling System™ has been called the most powerful method of ethical persuasion ever created, but it's not for everyone."

The build-up is: "The Strategic Marketing Coach Selling System™ has been called the most powerful method of ethical persuasion ever created."

The take-away is: "but it's not for everyone."

The build-up captures the imagination of the prospect, while the take-away entices the prospect to want to know more. The prospect then begins selling you on why they would be interested.

Crossover Moves allow you to sit back and watch your prospects sell you on the merits of your product or service from their point of view. When a prospect makes a case for what you are selling, it becomes difficult for them to reverse course and act disinterested. You build up, then take away; build up, then take away... and if you do that long enough, prospects sell themselves.

Crossover Moves are the opposite of traditional selling methods. Because of this, the prospect is kept off balance. They cross-over from the expected to the unexpected.

Fade Moves

Fade Moves can bring negative prospects back into the sales process, or confirm the interest of a positive prospect. Here is an example of using a Fade Move with a negative prospect:

The prospect says, "We're pretty happy with our current supplier."

You say, "And you've made up your mind not to talk to anyone else {pause} for any reason?"

Can you see how the Fade Move brings the prospect back into the conversation?

Cushioning Statements

Cushioning Statements acknowledge what the prospect said before you ask a question (or use a Crossover or Fade move). Here are a couple of examples: OK. That makes sense. I understand.

Fat Words & Phrases

Fat Words are ambiguous words and phrases prospects use that need to be clarified. The most common phrase salespeople encounter is: "I'll keep it in mind." The best way to deal with these is to ask for clarification. You might say, "What exactly do you mean when you say, 'I will keep it in mind?'"

Head Fakes

The most common Head Fake we hear from prospects is: "I'm just looking." This is an automatic reaction to the question: "May I help you?" Instead of approaching a prospect in this way, make a statement of fact that the prospect cannot deny - then tie it to a question that will open the door to the pains and consequences of not doing business with you (as stated in the Bonding & Rapport section).

Objections

I don't have to tell you what these are. You encounter them in almost every selling situation. Once you begin to look at them as moves that prospects make that you counter within the sales process, they become much easier to deal with.

Although there are hundreds of maneuvers within the Strategic Marketing Coach Selling System™, there are generally only seven objections you will ever encounter in a selling situation. You only need to have seven moves to counter those objections to close any sale.

THE SCIENCE OF ETHICAL PERSUASION

Question: If you have a choice of prospect to call on (positive, negative, or neutral), with which prospect do you have the least chance of closing the sale?

Welcome to Pendulum Theory, the foundation on which the Strategic Marketing Coach Selling System™ is built.

See page 10 for exclusive reader-only FREE offers!

Pendulum Theory is based upon Newton's First Law of Motion, which states: **An object in motion tends to stay in motion, and an object at rest tends to stay at rest.**

Here's how it works. Imagine a pendulum that swings back and forth from left to right, or right to left. When the pendulum swings to the far right, you are at 3:00 and are dealing with an extremely positive prospect. When the pendulum swings to the far left, you are at 9:00 and dealing with an extremely negative prospect. When the pendulum is at rest, you are at 6:00 and dealing with a neutral prospect.

During the sales process, the prospect will swing back and forth along the pendulum. For the most part, you want to stay to the left of the prospect (negative). By doing this, the prospect will naturally swing to the positive side of the pendulum. Your job is to get the person to swing far enough to one side of the pendulum that they will make a decision. A prospect will only make a committed decision when they have reached either the far right or far left of the pendulum (and stay there).

Pendulum Theory is very powerful, and is true sales psychology. It keeps the prospect emotional throughout the call, and produces amazing results. Never forget, people buy based on emotion and justify their decision with logic.

In the examples below, you will see how we deal with each of the prospect types. Please understand - this is just one way of approaching each prospect - there are hundreds of variations.

The Negative Prospect:

Let's assume in this situation the prospect is giving us signals that she is not going to buy.

You say, "I'm getting the feeling that this is of no interest to you...am I right?"

The prospect says, "No. I am very interested. I just have a couple of nagging questions."

Notice how the negative question moved the prospect to the positive side of the pendulum? We backed away from the prospect, and let her move toward us. The approach is low-key. It is the complete opposite of traditional selling. Subtle, but very effective.

Traditional selling methods recommend being enthusiastic. Overcome objections. I have two questions for you...how is that working for you? And, are you totally happy with your current results? Two Crossover Moves in a row.

The Positive Prospect:

The positive prospect says, "This is just what I've been looking for!"

Beware of the overly positive prospect. In this case, you are probably thinking you have a lay-down. Finally, an easy one. Don't get too excited yet. Forget what you've heard about close early, and close often. Never let an overly positive prospect take you out of your selling system.

Here is a safer way of handling the overly positive prospect.

You say, "Really! I would have guessed that you weren't interested. What did I miss?"

You have just invited the prospect to tell you why this is just what she was looking for. In essence, the prospect will sell herself.

This positive prospect is either going to become more positive (and sold), or swing over to the negative side (which is perfectly okay, because we have them moving). No matter what direction they move, we are raising their emotion level, which gets them closer to making a committed decision.

The Neutral Prospect:

What about the neutral prospect? They are actually the hardest to sell because you have to get them in motion. The safest way to get a neutral prospect in motion is to move to their left and open with a negative statement.

You say, "This may not be of any interest to you."

The prospect says, "Actually I am interested."

Now you are off to the races. If you can use Pendulum Theory whenever you are in a selling situation, you will be well on your way to getting your prospects to close themselves.

THE STRATEGIC MARKETING
COACH SELLING SYSTEM™

In this chapter, we've talked about a system with different components that make you a more persuasive salesperson. Most people don't like being thought of as a salesperson, and people definitely do not like being sold. With this system, the prospect actually closes him or herself, and you act as a facilitator that moves them toward making a decision. Once you learn it, being a highly-effective ethical persuader will come naturally to you.

See page 10 for exclusive reader-only FREE offers!

FREE!
Continue Your Learning And
Business-Building Online:
www.MDMSbonus.com

CHAPTER TEN

The 10 Commandments of Power Positioning

The Proven, Simple and Profitable Alternative to Old Fashioned Prospecting

Michel Fortin

Copywriter, Author, Speaker,
and Consultant

A direct response copywriter for more than 15 years, Michel Fortin has an uncanny knack for writing clearly, persuasively and vibrantly.

His track record speaks for itself. In the last few years, he was instrumental in selling several millions of dollars worth of products and services for a wide variety of clients stretching hundreds of different and unrelated industries.

One of his salesletters sold a record-breaking $1.08 million online on the first day. But that didn't stop him. A few months later, another salesletter for a completely different product generated over $1.04 million in three weeks.

As an in-demand public speaker and consultant, Michel often talks at conferences, bootcamps and seminars around the world — charging as much as $1,500 to $5,000 a seat to attend!

Today, Michel is the author of several books, including the freely available *The 10 Commandments of Power Positioning* and *Power Positioning Dotcom*, as well as his DVD, *"How to Write Profit-Pulling Copy In 3 Simple Steps."*

Michel and his articles have appeared in over 500 publications, including Internet.com, Home Business Magazine, Web Promote, Wealth Building Magazine, Office.com, Marketing Power! and others. He publishes a free email newsletter, The Profit Pill.™ In it, he reveals copywriting tips, techniques and resources.

The Success Doctor
Ottawa, Ontario CA • 613-482-7636 • www.SuccessDoctor.com

Michel Fortin

The 10 Commandments of Power Positioning

The Proven, Simple and Profitable Alternative to Old Fashioned Prospecting

Long gone are the days of knocking on and knocking down doors to get business, let alone just to get people's attention. Long gone are the days of using the phone to such an extent that your ear starts to shape itself into a phone's headset. And long gone are the days of bruised knees that came as a result of constantly begging your customers to give you mere table scraps of their business.

In short, prospecting is out. And positioning is in!

You're about to learn 10 core principles based on my "Power Positioning" concept—a set of powerfully effective strategies that have made tons of profitable business for many entrepreneurs and professionals like you. And, whether you want a little or a lot more business, these techniques are so simple that they can be easily applied by both types of entrepreneurs.

TOP-OF-MIND AWARENESS

First, you must understand the concept behind this chapter. In today's society, we have experienced two major shifts that have almost completely revolutionized the entire business landscape.

The first is increased competition. The mere fact that business is becoming increasingly hypercompetitive is an understatement. Businesses, particularly home-based businesses and self-employed professionals, are growing at an explosive rate.

For a person or business to remain in business, marketing strategies must be such that it places them at the top of prospects' minds at all times. The goal is to be the one from whom they choose to buy or with whom they choose to do business -- among all possibilities.

"Power Positioning" is a term I've coined that stands for a perfect blend of the art of positioning and the science of direct response—the result of creating top-of-mind awareness in order to become a powerful response magnet.

The following commandments all reflect this concept...

COMMANDMENT #1: THOU SHALL NOT COPY

The common problem in all advertising and marketing is the sheer fact that everything just seems to look like everything else. If one copies another company, let alone another company's promotion, it only serves as a reminder of one's competition!

As Earl Nightingale once said, "Don't copy, create!" Be unique. Be original. Be special. Be different. In fact, be so different that, if possible, your name or the name of your firm as well as the services you deliver become generic in the minds of prospects.

Have you ever heard a doctor say: "Take two acetylsalicylic acid tablets and call me in the morning"? What about facial tissue, cotton swab or adhesive bandage? Of course not. It's Aspirin, Kleenex, Q-Tip and Band-Aid.

Xerox, FedEx, Velcro, Kwik Kopy and Quick Lube stick like glue in the mind. This is possible because many of these firms created not only a new product but also a whole new category to place them in.

Remember to look at every aspect of your business, whether it's answering your phone, writing your invoices, mailing your brochures, even handing out your business cards. Every business activity should emphasize in some way your uniqueness!

COMMANDMENT #2: THOU SHALL APPOINT THYSELF

My early consulting career focused on doctors, cosmetic surgery and medical practices. I often asked doctors this question: "Look at the leaders in your specific field -- are they famous because they're busy, or are they busy because they're famous?"

See page 10 for exclusive reader-only FREE offers!

This is the power of self-appointment.

One of my favorite marketing gurus is author and speaker Dan Kennedy. He stresses, "You don't need someone else's permission to become successful."

Yet, many fail at creating top-of-mind awareness by drowning their image in a known category. They try to be better than everyone.

Everybody knows who is the first in some category or another, but rarely do people remember who's second or third. So, if there's no category you can be first in, create one!

Make it impossible for others to copy you.

COMMANDMENT #3: THOU SHALL MAKE THE ORDINARY EXTRAORDINARY

Do you offer an extraordinary product or service, or do you offer an ordinary one? Even if the service you provide is customary, traditional, and probably offered by your competition, you should make it appear unique just as well.

Remember, perception is more powerful than truth. Perception generally falls into one of three categories. The first is "customary," the second is "assumed," and the third is "unique."

The Customary

You might be a bookkeeper offering an income tax service as part of your portfolio -- one that is widely offered by most bookkeepers these days. But don't just leave it like that. Say "Ask us about our special 'Total Tax Tranquility' service."

The Assumed

Speaking of mechanics, are you a mechanic and, as normal practice, offer free estimates? If you are a mechanic, you might call your free estimate, "The Hassle Freedom Formula" or the "No Greater than Guesstimate Estimate." Or your tagline could even be something like, "Where Smiles and Estimates are Free!"

In other words, you're turning an assumed product or service into an assured one in the minds of people. And in this day and age where people no longer have time to search for specific information, when they'll need a free estimate your name will pop into their minds instantaneously.

The Unique

Above all, you may still be offering some very special or unique product or service that your competition doesn't offer at all. If so, that's great! However, don't just leave it to a vague title or description. Put a name on it, even if it's not entirely new.

In fact, while having a unique product or service beats the previous two categories in creating top-of-mind awareness, it doesn't have to be entirely new. It can be copied and customized in such a way that it appears unique or new. According to Brian Tracy in his program "The Psychology of Selling," many people have made fortunes by simply improving a current product by merely 10%, yet packaged it in a different way.

COMMANDMENT #4: THOU SHALL FIND MORE WITH LESS

The most common mistake newcomers to business make is to think that by expanding their portfolio they will secure more business. Conversely, they think that by narrowing their market they will also narrow their chances of getting more business. In either case, nothing can be further from the truth.

The truth of the matter is the fact that specializing and narrowing your focus as much as possible will increase your likelihood of getting more business.

An accountant specializing in car dealerships will get more business than a general accountant will. An advertising consultant specializing in print media strictly for home furnishing stores will get more business than a typical advertising agent will.

If you're new to business or hesitant about narrowing your focus since you want the ability to offer different products or services, focus on a specific niche to start, or create one as a "division" of your main business or focus. Then, as business creates enough cashflow and confidence, consider expanding.

COMMANDMENT #5: THOU SHALL DIVIDE AND CONQUER

If you're a specialist in your field -- which I hope you are after reading this book -- and you offer only one type of service, you can

See page 10 for exclusive reader-only FREE offers!

expand from within by dividing your core (your product or service) into multiple, smaller components.

This achieves three things. 1) It doesn't take away from your category or specialization. 2) It increases your hit ratio when targeting clients, since some of them might be interested in your entire package while others may be interested in only a portion of it. And 3) it increases the aura of expertise you project because you refrain from spreading yourself too thinly.

Let's say you are a programmer and you offer consulting work. For instance, you may provide consulting, research, programming, implementation, testing, hardware installation, training, customization, upgrades, licensing -- and the list can go on and on.

Ultimately, remember that by dividing your core you will paradoxically multiply your chances of getting more business. Each one of your "divisions" can cater to its own individual niche. If you own and operate multiple niches, when added up they can become very profitable for you.

COMMANDMENT #6: THOU SHALL TAKE IT STEP BY STEP

A mistake businesspeople often make is trying to sell their company directly in every communication they produce. They utilize institutional advertising (or what I call "blind branding").

They think that by selling themselves right in the ad, with clever punches and ideas, they will get not only an immediate response but also immediate business. This often backfires.

A better concept is direct-response marketing. It is a process in which businesses seek an immediate response as a result of their marketing. While it is often used to sell in the immediate sense, many use this technique to offer a free report, item, or service.

The idea is to have people come to you rather than you to them. I personally prefer the "free report" style of lead generation. The incentive doesn't have to relate directly to what you do. As long as it logically appeals to the same target market, you're on your way.

What can you offer prospects to arouse their curiosity and interest? What can you give away for free to entice them to get more, identifying themselves to you as interested, qualified "prospects?"

COMMANDMENT #7: THOU SHALL SPEAK SOFTLY BUT CARRY A BIG STICK

The next step is where to advertise. The trick is to have your ad noticed and read by such a specific group of people as much, as often, and as effectively as possible.

General publications won't do that. And they cost more money per lead generated.

Specialized publications, on the other hand, have the distinction of appealing to a specific audience and thus increase the chances of it being noticed as well as read. Why? If one newspaper has a readership of 100,000 but only 25,000 fits into your demographics, where another has only 40,000 readers but all of which fits into your demographics (because the publication is specialized), which one do you think will give you the greatest response?

There are numerous publications for specific people or with specialized topics. As long as the readership somehow logically fits into your target market, this is where you will get the greatest bang for your marketing buck.

COMMANDMENT #8: THOU SHALL BECOME A CELEBRITY

Once you become the leader in your category or in your unique area of expertise, you need to be known as such. And one of the most effective ways to do this is through publicity.

Publicity is different than advertising. Your goal is to get yourself known as an expert in your field.

Publicity is far more credible than advertising, since it comes from an "objective" third party. If you have narrowed your focus to a very specific, highly specialized field, publicity will come easy to you. The media loves to receive information from people who are uniquely qualified in their specialty.

Write articles for your local newspaper, or in the very least in the op-ed section. Send news releases to all the TV, newspaper, and radio stations in at least your area. Offer free seminars during fundraisers for non-profit or not-for-profit organizations. Offer to speak at luncheons, clubs, and organizations such as the Rotary.

Get out and about! Get others to know you and talk about you.

See page 10 for exclusive reader-only FREE offers!

COMMANDMENT #9: THOU SHALL
SEEK OUT AND SPREAD OUT

Whether it's local directories, specialty directories, occupation-specific registries, industry or trade directories, yellow pages, search engines, Internet directories, or trade publications, you should seek them out and list your company in as many of them as you can. The trick is to spread out. Essentially, being everywhere.

This also applies to the Internet, with search engines and online directories. Try to be on as many of the major search engines as possible, and also try to spread out as much as possible among them using keywords that appeal to your market.

You want to be in front of your prospects often, but more importantly when they decide to buy from you. In other words, spread yourself thin. Don't be big. Be small. But be everywhere!

COMMANDMENT #10: THOU SHALL
MAKE THY NET WORK

I hate networking. I hate it because, in my experience, it hasn't brought me anything substantial in return. You're probably saying right now, "What? Is he crazy? Has he lost his mind?"

But wait. Hear me out. Networking isn't a bad concept.

However, here's the problem. Having a network and having a networking system are two entirely separate things. When you're only networking, for instance, often people will want something in return or else they will either stop sending you clients or simply lose interest (if you don't take the time to recognize their efforts, and that's if you have any time left at all).

So, how can you reward your network? Better yet, how can you turn your network into a networking system? The answer is by developing a network of strategic marketing alliances... or marketing joint ventures.

In my experience, I have found that they mainly fall into three major categories. The first is what I call the info-network, the second is the auto-network and the third, the intra-network.

Info-Networking

The information-based network is one in which a strategic marketing alliance is created in which information is exchanged in some form or another between parties. Basically, that information includes qualified leads that both you and your alliance share, or information about each other that is promoted to each party's target market or clientele (also known as "cross-promotion").

Auto-Networking

Auto-networking is the process of creating referral-sources that automatically supply you with good quality leads, automatically, without you having to lift a finger. Things like brochure stands, posters, flyers, coupons and business cards can be placed at the offices of potential referral-sources.

Intra-Networking

Think of intracorporate divisions, Intranets and intrapreneurs (e.g., employees owning a portion of their employer's company). "Intra-anything" simply means two or more parts of a whole that are independent but also inter-dependent.

It's like a network "within a network."

For instance, a restaurant makes an arrangement with a local gas station to offer coupons to each client that comes to pump gas. They were given the permission to hang posters in the station, leave menus at the counter, and place fridge magnets on the pumps. For every 10 coupons the restaurant received, the employees at the station were given a free meal.

Altogether, info-networking, auto-networking and intra-networking are powerful tools to help you create good referral-sources that never stop working. The idea is nonetheless to network but to do so wisely so as to be able to create as many leads and clients as possible with the least amount of effort.

Don't network. Make your net work for you!

FREE!

**Continue Your Learning And
Business-Building Online:
www.MDMSbonus.com**

CHAPTER ELEVEN

Using Gift Cards To Grow Your Business

Can Gift Cards Really Be The Most Profitable Item You Sell?

John Gilvary
Author, Speaker & Consultant

"Markets are changing faster than ever. In order to stand out in a crowd of me-too competitors, you must open your mind to new ideas", says John Gilvary, MBA.

As a marketing strategist, freelance copywriter and professional speaker, John helps forward-thinking business owners restructure (or sometimes just fine tune) their marketing strategies, tactics and efforts to grow their business enterprises. Nothing you can do will grow your business faster, or more profitably.

John Gilvary's strategies for growing your business include:

- How to incorporate gift cards into your marketing mix (even if yours is an on-line business)
- Customized marketing strategy makeovers
- Direct response style copywriting for more effective, and accountable, advertising
- Connecting you with the service providers who best fit your business

Castle Rock Publishing
Discovery Bay, CA • 877-418-3390 • www.jgilvary.com

John Gilvary

Using Gift Cards To Grow Your Business

Can Gift Cards Really Be The Most Profitable Item You Sell?

Most businesses are missing out on one of the most profitable, yet often misunderstood items they can sell. Some of these business owners already have gift cards... yet were never taught how to use them for maximum business-building effect. Other entrepreneurs don't offer gift cards because they were never informed of their profit potential in the first place. At last, you have the solutions for your business, regardless of which category you fit into. That's because...

In this chapter, I'll share some of my favorite and most powerful marketing strategies for turning gift cards into a business-booming marketing machine.

But first, allow me to set the table with some grounding information on gift cards and how to measure their beneficial effects on your business. Fair enough? OK. Let's get started.

What is a gift card?

A gift card is basically a plastic version of a gift certificate. It is similar in size to a credit card and allows you to store value, usually with a magnetic stripe, or in the case of a "smart" card, with a small computer chip. These plastic stored value cards are completely replacing the paper gift certificate, for many reasons. (They now represent about 80% of the gift card/gift certificate market according to Card Marketing magazine.)

Why are they replacing gift certificates?

Some of the strategies I will share with you will work with gift certificates, just as they do with gift cards. Here are some of the reasons why gift cards work better.

- Converting your gift certificate system to a gift card system typically increases this type of gift sale by 50-300%, depending on how you market them. The retail industry average is 75%.

- Plastic cards increase security, cutting fraud because, unlike certificates, cards are nearly impossible to counterfeit.

- Cards speed up the handling process. This adds to your bottom line by reducing labor costs by 30-50%, according to Integrated Solutions for Retailers.

- Gift cards can process through most modern credit card terminals, eliminating the labor-intensive paper shuffling required by a certificate system.

- They can be displayed out in the open, encouraging purchases, yet holding no value until "loaded" on the point-of-sale (POS) equipment... and then only *after* the customer pays you.

- Consumers prefer plastic cards because they are easier to purchase and are far more convenient to use and carry than their paper counterparts. When you make it more convenient, they'll buy more and use them more often.

- Chain Pooling-if you have multiple locations, you will love the advantages of "pooling" with plastic gift cards. That's because certificates or store credit slips issued at one store and redeemed at another can create a reconciliation migraine. My gift card processor provides automated reports that reconcile these intra-chain transactions for you.

- Today, gift cards are the most popular form of gift to give and receive among young people, and their sales presence is powerful enough to garner them exclusive space in retail stores.

- Merchants can increase sales by simply eliminating paper certificates hidden in the cash drawer and displaying gift cards on sales racks.

See page 10 for exclusive reader-only FREE offers!

- Your clients can add value to the cards or use the remaining balance toward the purchase of a larger value item.

- Your processing company should be able to combine gift and loyalty capacity within the same cards. (A loyalty card encourages repeat buying from your clients.) A 10% Improvement in Loyalty = 25% to 80% Increase in your Net Profit.

Now that you have a good understanding of the gift card vehicle, it's time to dig into…

THE LIFETIME VALUE OF A CLIENT…OR HOW TO KNOW HOW WELL YOUR MARKETING IS WORKING

In order for you to really appreciate the value of any marketing strategy or campaign, you must first be familiar with the value of a client… specifically, the lifetime value of a new client, sometimes called "marginal net worth."

Most business owners don't fully appreciate the value of a client over his entire relationship life with the business. Many businesses make this costly, yet common mistake. Here is how it works…

Let's say you have a retail store, selling fashion clothing. (Although the same principles apply if you sell sporting goods, jewelry, art, office supplies, or you own a restaurant, spa, or any type of business that generates repeat business.)

So you run an ad in the local newspaper about a sale. Customer Sue Jones comes in because of that ad. Do you know what it cost you to get her to visit your store? It is easy to find out if you capture and track that result. How?

You can ask a better question than most retailers ask. Instead of asking "Can I help you" which tends to generate the same automatic response… (Yeah, say it with me…)

"No thanks, I'm just looking."

Simply ask the new client **"which ad brought you to us today?"** Keep track of the visitors who saw your ad in the local paper and divide the cost of running the ad by the number of people who visit you as a result. You'll also want to know how many of these pairs of feet through your door resulted in new clients. Pretty simple math-yet rarely applied. You will need to know that information when determining the worth of the ads you're running.

Another valuable number you will need is the sales and profits you receive from that new client. How many times she will return and buy again over her lifetime. And how much she will spend on her average visit. When you have these data, you will be able to determine the lifetime value of a client. Only then, will you know what you can spend on advertising and know if you are getting your money's worth from your ads.

Back to our example...

Sue Jones comes in and buys $100 worth of clothing during her first visit. Now, lets say that your experience tells you she will return 6 times a year for the next 5 years, before she moves out of your service area, or no longer buys clothes, or she finds a competitor she likes better... or stops shopping with you for whatever reason.

This means that the average new client will give you 5 years x 6 visits per year, or 30 visits at $100 sales each, plus your initial sale of another $100. That is a total sale amount of $3,100. If you are at keystone, or your profit margin is 50%, that means you have a gross profit of $1,550 for every new client.

So if you run an ad for $5,000 and it brings in 50 new clients, you paid $100 to gain each new client. Since you only made $50 on each first sale, (for a total of $2,500), you might think the ad didn't work. That's because you initially invested $5,000 to bring in a gross profit of $2,500.

But knowing the lifetime value of a new client, you realize that you're $1,500 ahead of the game, on average, per new client. When you multiply that by 50 new clients you got from that ad, you made $75,000 because of that ad. Or...

$1,550	gross profit per new client
-50	ad cost per new client
$1,500	profit after ad cost (per new client)
x 50	new clients from the ad
$75,000	**lifetime value of new clients from the ad**

That equates to a return of $15.00 (over a 5-year life) for every $1.00 you invested in that campaign.

Your numbers will vary. Every business is different. That's why you must run the numbers for your business to use this formula accurately. Some businesses have a lifetime client value of a few hundred to over a million dollars. It may surprise you to realize that a good,

See page 10 for exclusive reader-only FREE offers!

sit-down restaurant, with a liquor license, can easily have a marginal net worth, or lifetime value of $50,000 or more for a new client.

> In a study by Kaleidoscope Media Group, some restaurants have identified clients who eat out 3-5 times a week. They found that some families of successful households spend $100 each time they eat out and frequent their favorite restaurants for as long as 10 years. This gives them a lifetime value of over $100,000. Here's an eye opener for so many business owners. Do you treat your new clients as if they are worth $50,000 over their lifetime? $100,000?
>   What would happen if you did?

There are also ways to improve those numbers. Improving your copy, for example, will get each ad to bring in more clients. You can also implement strategies that will get them to spend more each time they visit and come back to you more often.

I've identified eight ways that you can benefit from using gift cards in your business.

"Super 8" Gift Card Benefits

1. Breakage
2. Ticket lift
3. Return credit for merchandise-encourage repeat traffic and upsells
4. Incentives instead of discounting
5. Loyalty
6. Pro-active marketing
7. Secondary market
8. Tracking-3rd party proof of client activity-exit strategy

I only have space to fully explain two of the eight ways in this chapter, but will happily send a free report to any reader who asks for one. This will include all eight ways, in detail.

Let me explain the first two ways to benefit from gift cards here.

One benefit is what is known as "breakage". Breakage occurs when someone buys a gift card for say $50 and spends less. Say they spend only $35 of their $50 gift card. You just got $15 of pure profit in addition to the $17.50 of keystone markup, nearly doubling your profit on that transaction. Breakage will typically average 14% of your total gift card sales… and of those customers, a full 40% leave balances of more than $5, according to a study by Synergistics.

A second benefit of using gift cards is known as "ticket lift." This is the opposite of breakage. Ticket lift occurs, for example, when the same customer with a $50 gift card ends up spending $70. This increases your sales and profits accordingly. How prevalent is ticket lift? In a study commissioned by ValueLink, some 61% of consumers said they usually spend more than the initial value of their gift card. Consumers typically spend at least 40% more than the card's original value.

Keep these two high-profit benefits of gift cards in mind, while you consider the following strategies.

APPLYING GIFT CARD STRATEGIES TO LOWER YOUR CLIENT ACQUISITION COSTS AND LEVERAGE YOUR CLIENT'S LIFETIME VALUE

So let's say a newspaper ad will bring in customers at $100 a piece and that is a good deal for you. **Here's a strategy to get that same client in the door for under $50.**

Strategy #1: Direct Mail For New Clients

Get a list of your prime prospects in your market area. Are they new homeowners?… do they have a home that is 10, 20, 50 years old? Are they of a particular age range? Do they have children? What are their children's ages? What is their household income level? Which neighborhoods do they live in? The best list will be of people who tend to influence others. The specifics of the most desirable list will depend on your particular product/market.

There are various list sources… some may surprise you. For example, one of my clients is a company that provides their clients with up to 1,000 names and addresses per month of new homeowners in their market area. **They do this free for a year**, as an incentive to do business with them. If your business sells to other businesses (B2B), they will provide a similar list of new businesses in your market area. Email me at johng@jgilvary.com, if you would like more information.

See page 10 for exclusive reader-only FREE offers!

OK, so now that you have your list of ideal prospects in your market area. Simply send them a letter, enclosing an actual live gift card. How about this... you send out 1,000 letters, enclosing gift cards with a mystery value. For example out of the 1,000 letters, 900 can have a gift card valued at $25; 50 valued at $50, 49 valued at $100 and 1 card valued at $500. Here's the catch: they must come into your store to find out how much their card is worth. You can restrict the card so that no cash refunds are available. Let's run the numbers.

900 times $25	=	$22,500
50 times $50	=	$2,500
49 times $100	=	$4,900
1 times $500	=	$500
Total prize fund	=	**$30,400**

But wait, your cost is keystone, or 50% of that, or $15,200. If everyone who gets the letter comes in and spends only the amount of their card winnings, it cost you $15.20 per new client. That is worst-case scenario.

Let me tell you what will more likely happen. As a minimum, you will see profits from breakage and ticket lift, as I mentioned above.

If you like this particular strategy, but your cash flow situation prevents you from running this test, contact me at johng@jgilvary.com for ways to make it happen for you.

Strategy #2: Company JV

You can capitalize on another target market by joint venturing with a local leading business... maybe a major employer who wants to reward their employees. Instead of a Thanksgiving turkey, maybe the employees would like to get a gift card from your business.

By providing gift cards, the business gets to reward their employees, while avoiding the costs. By sending them to your business, you now have an implied endorsement from your future client's boss.

This strategy will work whether you sell the gift cards to the employer at full price, at a generous discount, or even if you give them away... because of the lifetime value of the clients. (You are getting new clients for a small acquisition cost.) You are growing your own client list, for a modest investment.

Strategy #3: Other Joint Venture Candidates

Or maybe there is a good possibility of teaming up with a local business that caters to your same type of client… but is not competing with you. For example, maybe you sell apparel but not shoes to the teen market and a business down the street, or on the other end of the mall, sells shoes to the same market. You can strike a deal that packages a gift card with a purchase. "Spend $200 on clothing this weekend and we'll give you a $25 gift card to Funky Shoes." Then reciprocate with Funky Shoes for a similar deal.

HOW TO SELL MORE GIFT CARDS… VIRTUALLY GUARANTEEING A MASSIVE ROI

- At the POS, merchandising of the cards is the biggest factor in making or breaking a gift card program. If they're not available or accessible at the POS, not many will sell

- The amount of time and money spent on creative promotion is important, and the look of the card is important, but merchandising is the key.

- The beauty is that they don't take up much space, and you can generate hundreds of dollars a day from the same spot you sell 50-cent packs of gum.

- But the big retailers have realized that this is a preferred product, in many cases the number one or two seller in their stores.

HOW DO YOU SELECT A GIFT CARD SERVICE PROVIDER?

- Look for a provider with industry experience
- A proven platform for transactions and marketing,
- An understanding of the multiple retail/restaurant markets, and
- Overall knowledge and ability to market gift cards to your consumers.

In short, you want someone to help you establish and market your gift cards, who has done it before.

See page 10 for exclusive reader-only FREE offers!

FREE!

**Continue Your Learning And
Business-Building Online:
www.MDMSbonus.com**

CHAPTER TWELVE

Let Go & Grow!

How to Do Less and Accomplish More In Your Business With Profitable Outsourcing

Marc Goldman

"The King of Ecommerce"

Marc Goldman is the CEO of Goldbar Enterprises, a visionary e commerce software and digital media company based out of White Plains, New York.

Along with his wife Terry, he founded Goldbar back in 1994. They turned their blood, sweat and tears (and $30,000.00 in credit card debt) into a 7-figure a year enterprise with a full time staff and offices around the globe.

Marc is acutely aware of the typical problems of small business owners (Lack of Capital, Lack of Prospects, Lack of Customers) and has consequently developed a Paint by Numbers, 5-Step System to DRAMATICALLY INCREASE the profits of ANY business using a combination of killer Online and Offline Marketing techniques.

Marc Goldman can teach you at least 7 unique and affordable solutions to your business problems! Here is just a small sampling of what you will learn when you listen to Marc:

- How to generate more revenue than you could ever imagine by tapping into the hidden assets buried in your business.
- Four innovative, proprietary techniques on how to maximize revenues from your existing customers
- A proven system to automatically get referrals from your friends and customers
- Super simple (and really slick) ways to convert site visitors (and store browsers) into REAL, hard core prospects

Goldbar Enterprises, LLC
White Plains, NY • 914-422-0290 • www.goldbar.net

Marc Goldman

Let Go & Grow!

How to Do Less and Accomplish More In Your Business With Profitable Outsourcing

I want to ask you to take a few moments for some introspection. Take a deep breath, grab a cup of coffee (or tea), turn off the phone, shut off your email and your Instant Messengers and lock yourself in a dark room.

We are going to do a business intervention...

The intervention starts with me asking you some pointed questions. The results of this intervention working for you are solely dependent on just how honest you can be with yourself.

Ready? Ok, let's go:

1. Do you have more money than time?

2. Do you own 3 or more "intend to" products or services? "Intend to" is when you buy something and "intend to do it (i.e. read or use it) later." Of course you never seem to get around to it and sometimes you even end up getting charged for months for things you never actually make use of.

3. Do you have a business (or part of a business) that you know you could grow online if you just had the money to hire someone else to implement all the cool automation that you see others using?

4. Are you sick of watching what seems like EVERY OTHER business grow to new heights using online marketing while

your business remains stagnant just because you don't have the time or resources to figure out what it takes to drive traffic to your site, convert visitors to prospects, and then convert prospects to sales that buy and buy again (many times without ANY intervention at all on your part)?

5.   Are you a business owner, entrepreneur, speaker, coach or consultant focused on doing whatever it is that you love and you just wish you had someone else to take over all the tech stuff?

If you answered yes to any of the questions above, then this chapter is for you. This is your intervention.

If you are like most people who are involved in a small business and you didn't answer yes to one of the questions above, let me be frank with you - I think you are probably lying to yourself.

As a successful small business owner myself I can attest to the fact that there just aren't enough hours in the day to do everything that I want to do with my business.

And when you're a 1 or 2 person show, as most of us start out in business; it never seems feasible to hire an employee does it?

You always figure: "I can do that better...let me just do it myself."

That's part of the "serial entrepreneur's" mentality. We always grab the bull by the horns and just "do it ourselves".

And yet I can tell you, from my very own experience, that you will NEVER achieve true growth in your business until you get someone else to take over tasks that free you up to focus on doing what you love or are best at.

A business will always (assuming it has REAL profit potential to start with) grow when it has added employees or outsourced tasks to outside experts.

Businesses throughout the years have proven time and again that adding just 1 employee could free up a business owner to do whatever it is they want to do:

- Market the business more aggressively
- Focus on creating new products and/or services (or perfecting their existing product line).

See page 10 for exclusive reader-only FREE offers!

- Spend more time speaking and or consulting

- Have more free time to use however they like

It's what Robert Kiyosaki describes as the difference between Owning a business and Working in your business.

Most people- even though they "own a business" become employees and not really business owners.

Those who leverage Other People's Time will become free of the parts of their business that keep them down and will therefore be free to focus on doing what they love.

You can get more of every resource you have except for time so therefore you really need to utilize Other People's Time to work on tasks that are necessary for the success and day to day operations of your business.

So why don't more people just hire someone to work in their business?

Frankly, I think most people believe that they are:

1. Unable to afford to hire someone else

2. Better at doing the work themselves as opposed to letting someone else have control of it

Now for some people, issue # 1 may be entirely true. They may be just starting out or they may be unable or unwilling to see the profitability of bringing someone on board who has the knowledge and skills they lack (or enjoys doing tasks that they don't).

Issue #2 is an entirely different story. This has more to do with letting go and allowing a facet of your business to be in the hands of others (something which many people are completely unable to do).

But what if I told you that the absolute BEST way to grow your business was to focus on what you do best and allow others to handle everything else.

And I am not just guessing or speculating or theorizing when I tell you this.

This has been a fact in our business life.

For example, when my wife and I started our business together 10 years ago (we provide ecommerce software that other businesses can use to grow their business), we used to do ABSOLUTELY everything ourselves:

- We did the marketing

- We did our own customer support

- We dabbled in programming

- We set up all the technical backend services our business needed to run

- We did all our own copywriting

- We basically lived and breathed EVERY single aspect of our business.

And one thing always rang true:

We were always overstressed, over tired, over busy and our business was just not producing the revenue we needed to make our blood, sweat and tears and years of sacrifice really pay off.

But we could see no other way out of it.

You see, we were convinced that no one could do it better (and frankly we weren't convinced the money we would have to spend on an employee would be worth it).

And this continued for many, many years.

Until the day we almost completely broke down due to extreme exhaustion and stress.

And we were forced to make a change in our lives.

Before I tell you what happened, let me tell you that I am writing this chapter because the inner working of entrepreneurs interests me greatly.

As a matter of fact I have made this part of my life's study.

For example, I love watching TV shows about entrepreneurs.

My interest has a lot to do with the fact that I too am a entrepreneur and I love to find out what similar traits I share with other small business successes (and I also like to learn whatever I can from those who have failed before me).

Without fail, the one trait that I find most often repeating itself in successful entrepreneurs is:

PASSION!

They do what they love.

See page 10 for exclusive reader-only FREE offers!

Because they are doing what they love, they have the will, the determination and the intestinal fortitude to make it through the tough times that affect every business regardless of their location in the world.

The ones who don't have the passion are the ones who muddle through, just getting by (or failing) and who will happily re-enter the workforce if and when their business fails (and it most certainly will).

But doing what you love involves much more than just having a passion for your chosen career path. Some of us are lucky - we get paid for doing things we love or have a natural talent for.

Imagine being able to soar high into the sky and slam down a basketball with power and authority like Lebron James (and get paid millions for doing so). Imagine, being a dancer and getting paid to dance!

But what about when you have to:

Manage your finances

Handle daily administrative details

Clean

Cook

Not everyone loves those tasks.

So they become burdens. And when you associate burdens with your passion, then the passion starts to wane.

Now, back to the day that we almost collapsed from stress and overwork.

Our business was growing dramatically but our customer service demands were also increasing exponentially.

Now, I absolutely hate customer service.

Allow me to clarify - I love customers. They are the lifeblood of any business and I love helping our customers succeed with our ecommerce software and hosting, but I am certainly not the best one to deal with the tedious administrative tasks that make up a business.

So for years it made me completely miserable...

I dreaded it.

I probably kept our business down because I chose to involve myself in a part of my business that did not bring me ultimate joy.

When I finally made the decision to add on a customer support team to handle our customer support issues, not only did customer satisfaction rise much higher, but my own free time, personal enjoyment and productivity rose through the roof.

Because I removed that obstacle from my path, the one that was causing me pain and causing my passion to wane, I was able to "recapture the passion" and take my business to new heights with renewed vigor.

And then I was able to look at other tasks that we were involved in and hire staff to handle those as well:

We started to hire staff to handle:

- Technical Support
- Programming
- Website Design
- The Technical Management and Administration of our business

We even began to hire consultants and freelancers to:

- Write our sales material
- Consult on marketing
- Accounting and Financial issues
- Management of our corporate entity
- Legal matters

Each time we thought we couldn't afford it, we were proven wrong. Each time we hired someone we were able to improve our business, thanks to their help.

And coincidentally, each time our business makes a new hire, we get more and more free time.

Complete free time? No. But that is our choice. This business is ours and we like to remain involved on a day to day basis, talking to customers, making improvements in the system and bringing our vision to life.

So, this is it: the key to ultimate business happiness, success and productivity is to Do What YOU Love, let others handle the rest.

See page 10 for exclusive reader-only FREE offers!

SEEMS SIMPLE RIGHT?

Yet, every SINGLE day I find more and more people who run a business miserable and downtrodden and unable to pull themselves out of their rut (even though they may be in a business they are truly passionate about).

These people have yet to realize the ultimate joy that comes from focusing on what you love and handing off what you don't to others.

By the way I don't just go on my own experience as proof of this concept...

I also study my customers. In particular, I study the customers who cancel their account with our GoldbarOne Ecommerce Solution.

Since this software is the flagship product of our business, we study these responses very closely!

What I have discovered is this, even though people LOVE our service and consider it to be a powerful and user friendly ecommerce solution (their words not mine) the number ONE reason why people cancel their account:

They don't have the time to setup or administer the account themselves.

ISN'T THAT CRAZY?

We designed this service to be the ultimate small business problem solver. It contains everything you would need to run your online business (or bring your offline business online).

It helps you drive traffic to your website, turn that traffic into qualified prospects, turn more of those prospects into customers and then turn those customers into repeat buyers who come back to you time and time again.

I have talked to many a business owner and most of them would cut off their big toe for software that was capable of doing just that.

So, if that's the case, why aren't people climbing all over each other to sign up for our service and never, ever quit?

TIME

Simple as that.

They just don't have the time to set up the software, configure it for their business and integrate it into their website.

So - did we look at this and say – ok this is too big of a hurdle to overcome – guess it's time to close up shop?

No, we didn't...

Instead we figured out that we were really causing the problem. You see, we provided this awesome service that solves the problems of small businesses but then we overlooked one small detail:

Many people either don't want to do all this themselves or they simply don't have the time to do it themselves. So, after this business introspection, we realized that not only could we solve ANOTHER big problem of small businesses, we could do so in such a way that helped them benefit from using our ecommerce software producing a win-win situation for all involved.

And so our ExpertOne service was born. ExpertOne allows small businesses to "hire" our staff - the very same people who built GoldbarOne to analyze their business, set up and manage their account, and integrate our software into their websites (or build one from scratch for anyone who doesn't have one).

AND IT'S BEEN PRODUCING FABULOUS FEEDBACK FROM OUR USERS!

While we enjoy hearing the great comments, they really serve a purpose. They help us to illustrate the following point: if you want to turn a profitable online business idea into a reality, you should:

1. Focus your energies on whatever you are passionate about

2. Stop spending your precious time on tasks that others could do better

3. Look into hiring business help, not as an expense, but as an investment – one that can quickly produce dramatic returns for your business

Then and only then will you experience the true freedom of being a business owner. And to paraphrase Robert Kiyosaki - you always want to own your business, not let your business own you.

See page 10 for exclusive reader-only FREE offers!

FREE!
**Continue Your Learning And
Business-Building Online:
www.MDMSbonus.com**

CHAPTER THIRTEEN

Setting the Buying Criteria

How to Outmaneuver Your Competition and Convert More Prospects Into Customers

Ryan Healy

Direct Response Copywriter
& Marketing Strategist

"Business owners want to grow their businesses. I help them do that," says Ryan Healy.

As a direct response copywriter and marketing strategist, Ryan helps businesses generate "Mile High Results" from their marketing and advertising. The sales letters and marketing pieces he's crafted have already generated over $1 million in revenue.

Ryan's marketing strategies are highly effective and often create instant measurable increases in revenue for the clients he serves. Setting the buying criteria is just one of the many strategies he uses.

"Setting the criteria by which your prospects make a buying decision is very simple, yet very effective," says Healy. "It's low-hanging fruit. All you have to do is reach out and grab it."

You can visit Ryan online at www.HealyMarketing.com. Although his current clients keep him busy, he occasionally accepts new clients. You can read his buying criteria online at: www.HealyMarketing.com

Healy Marketing
Denver, CO • 720-344-7788 • www.HealyMarketing.com

Ryan Healy

Setting the Buying Criteria

How to Outmaneuver Your Competition and Convert More Prospects Into Customers

What if I told you there was a simple marketing strategy you could use to...

- Stop prospects from price shopping
- Convert more prospects to customers
- Pre-empt your competition

You'd want to know about it, right?

It gets even better. Because you don't have to be a great writer... or even a great marketer... to put this strategy to work in your business.

Just so you know how powerful this particular strategy is, let me tell you a story...

Before I became a freelance copywriter, I was the sole copywriter and online marketer for a well-known home schooling company.

I'd been mulling over how to use this strategy in the business. One morning, it clicked.

I spent four hours writing eight brief emails. I plugged them into our email system, posted the opt-in form on the web site, and waited to see what would happen.

The results?

Nearly 20,000 subscribers the first year and $115,168.09 in revenue.

The email series continued to produce revenue the second year, the third year, and on and on. All from less than a day's work. Pretty amazing, huh?

The strategy I used is called:

"SETTING THE BUYING CRITERIA"

A clearer way to say it is: setting the criteria by which your prospects make a buying decision.

In a nutshell, here is how it works. In your marketing material (emails, brochures, web sites, sales letters, etc.), you want to define what makes a good buying decision. And in your defining, you want to make sure that your company, product, or service is the only one that fits the definition.

This is setting the buying criteria.

When you set the criteria, you always want to do it in such a way that it excludes your competitors. They should not be able to qualify based on the criteria you've set.

This is why the criteria you use should always be exclusive to a greater or lesser degree.

Let me give you a quick example...

Assume for a moment you're a car manufacturer who specializes in sports cars. One of your criteria might read like this:

> "Whatever sports car you choose, make sure it has at least 250 horsepower. Any less and you'll be sacrificing speed, acceleration, and performance, all of which are critical to the pleasure you'll get from your new sports car."

You'll notice I set the criterion (250 horsepower) high enough that it eliminated some cars, but not so high that it eliminated all cars. No matter. The important thing is, I've narrowed the field.

See page 10 for exclusive reader-only FREE offers!

As we move on, we layer additional buying criteria:

"Once you've found a sports car that has at least 250 horsepower, you'll also want to make sure it has a 6-speed manual transmission. At least half the pleasure of a sports car is being in total control. An automatic transmission just won't cut it.

"Rear-wheel drive is a must for a true sports car. It gives you the best cornering power possible, without feeling like you're going to run off the road (as you might feel with a front-wheel drive vehicle).

"Also look for fully independent suspension, so you get the best road feel. Each wheel will move on its own, independent from the other wheels, giving you maximum traction and performance.

"Lastly, be picky about the kind of engine your sports car is equipped with. The best sports car engine is a boxer engine. It's perfectly balanced and produces no vibration. You can set a quarter directly on the engine while it is running and it will not fall off. Plus, boxer engines sit low to the ground and provide a lower center of gravity. Boxer engines can be found in flat-4, flat-6, and flat-12 configurations."

By shrewdly selecting these and possibly one or two additional criteria, I can make my sports car the only logical choice in a crowded market.

It's the same with your product. If you shrewdly define the criteria for buying, you'll create a scenario where your product is the only one that can possibly qualify. All competitive products will fall short.

WHY SETTING THE BUYING CRITERIA WORKS

Setting the buying criteria works for 3 powerful reasons:

1. You're seen as someone who can be trusted.

By telling your prospects what they should look for when they make a purchase-or conversely, telling them what to watch out for-you become a trusted advisor.

Your prospects believe you have their best interests at heart (and you do), so they are more likely to buy your product instead of the competition's.

2. You're letting your prospects come to their own conclusions.

When you set the buying criteria, you're not saying, "Buy my product because it's got X, Y, and Z."

Instead, you're indirectly guiding your prospects to the conclusion you want them to reach. You're saying, "When you make a purchase of this kind, make sure you get one with these things..."

Your prospects run down the checklist you've created and decide-on their own-that your product is the best choice.

3. You're doing something different.

If you examine your competition, you will be lucky if you find even one business taking advantage of this strategy. That makes it easy for you to stand out.

When your prospects see that you're looking out for them... and none of your competitors are... then it becomes exceptionally easy for you to turn them into customers. Prospects will be drawn to you, and will gladly give you their business.

See page 10 for exclusive reader-only FREE offers!

MORE EXAMPLES TO ILLUSTRATE BUYING CRITERIA

I don't know what your product is, so I'm going to use a few more examples to illustrate this process. So let's assume you're selling a high-end ski jacket.

Your criteria might look like this: zippered pockets, hood, removable liner, snow skirt, goggle pouch, season pass window, and a new proprietary waterproof/breathable fabric.

As you look at your competition, you find that nearly every single ski jacket on the market has "zippered pockets," and yet this is a feature that many skiers are looking for. "Zippered pockets" alone will not set you apart, so you go further.

Now you add the "hood" to your buying criteria. There are fewer ski jackets with both zippered pockets and a hood, but there are still many.

As you layer each additional feature of your high-end ski jacket, you notice there are fewer and fewer jackets that meet all the criteria you've defined.

By the time you add your proprietary waterproof/breathable fabric to the mix, there is only one ski jacket still in the running. It just so happens that it's the one you sell.

Is this starting to make sense?

If you run an accounting practice, your criteria may be: monthly statements (including P&L, trial balance, assets & liabilities, itemized expense reports, etc.), quarterly tax filing, daily backups to prevent lost data, and free tax planning twice a year.

If you sell a cleaning product, your criteria may be: kills bacteria in under 30 seconds, uses all-natural environmentally friendly ingredients, makes everything smell fresh, is packaged in an easy-to-use ergonomic container, and comes with a 90-day full money-back guarantee.

You may need more criteria; you may need less. Only you will know for your particular niche.

HOW TO DEFINE YOUR BUYING CRITERIA

To begin defining your buying criteria, list all of the features of your product or service. Do it quickly without thinking too much.

Simply write down all the different features that come to mind.

After you've captured all the features you can think of, review your list. Circle some of the core features that are always expected with a product or service like yours. Also circle the features that are the most unique.

Now you have the raw material you need to create a marketing piece that sets the buying criteria. The next step is in how you position these features-how you present them to your market.

This is a very important step. Position your criteria the wrong way and people will ignore you. Position your criteria the right way and new customers will flock to you.

HOW TO POSITION YOUR CRITERIA

When you set the buying criteria, there are a number of ways to position them. How you position them is important, and one may work better than another for your business.

The email series I wrote for the home schooling company was positioned like this: "The 7 Essentials That Will Inspire Your Children to Learn."

Many people (nearly 20,000 of them in the first year) subscribed purely out of curiosity. They wanted to know what the "7 Essentials" were.

With another client, I used a similar approach and wound up with "The 7 Essentials of Any Ecommerce System." If you're in the market for an ecommerce system, you'll want to find out what the "7 Essentials" are. After you're done reading, my client's system will be your only choice.

With my copywriting services, I position the criteria inside the sales letter. As you scroll down the site, you'll see a subhead that says, "The One Thing Your Copywriter Must Have."

In this case, the one thing is so rare, I don't feel the need to have a laundry list of criteria. Just the one is sufficient.

Another way to position your criteria is as a warning: "Don't Even Think About Buying _____ Until You Read This…" or "How to Buy a _____ Without Losing Your Shirt."

A warning is a more direct approach because it often acknowledges the prospects' desire to purchase a particular item, but the approach can still work very well.

See page 10 for exclusive reader-only FREE offers!

Joe Polish is famous in part for his method of setting the buying criteria in Consumer Awareness Guides. These little guides educate consumers about what they should look out for when they hire a carpet cleaner and other service professionals.

The possibilities for positioning your criteria are virtually limitless. Once you fully understand this strategy, you will begin to think of many ways to position your criteria.

But remember this: the most effective way to position your criteria will always be from an angle that educates and protects the consumer. You cannot say, "5 Reasons To Buy My Product."

Yawn.

Your prospect doesn't care about you or your product. At least not yet.

That's why you need to speak to your prospects with care and concern, as a trusted advisor to a dear friend. This is how you reach them. So make sure that you position your criteria with this in mind.

MAKE SURE YOU GIVE A <u>REASON WHY</u>

Before I turn you loose, I believe it's important for you to understand one more thing... that is, the importance of giving your prospects a reason why.

When you list out your criteria and position them in way that appeals to your prospects, you still need to make sure-with each and every criterion-that you are giving your prospects a believable reason why it's so important.

In my sports car illustration, I listed a reason why each criterion was important for the consumer to consider when choosing a sports car. I explained how the fully independent suspension was necessary for "maximum traction and performance." I mentioned that a 6-speed manual transmission was important because it gives you "total control."

If I had not given any reasons why these criteria are important for the consumer to consider, my case would have been very weak. The same holds true in real life. You must give your prospects a strong reason why.

Review your criteria. If you list a criterion for which there is no good reason why you've mentioned it, then it shouldn't be included. Get rid of it or find another criterion to replace it with.

EVALUATE YOUR MARKETING

As you evaluate your marketing, ask yourself this question: *Am I setting the criteria by which my prospects make a buying decision?*

If you are not, it is time for you to seriously consider how you might use this strategy in your business. It takes very little time to do and it is highly effective.

Once you implement it, you will stop prospects from price shopping, convert more prospects to customers, and-best of all-pre-empt your competition so you become the one and only logical choice, even if you're competing in a crowded market.

See page 10 for exclusive reader-only FREE offers!

FREE!
**Continue Your Learning And
Business-Building Online:
www.MDMSbonus.com**

CHAPTER FOURTEEN

Golden Handcuffs

How to Lock-In Customer Loyalty With Superior Service!

Andy Jacobs

Entrepreneur, Author & Speaker

Raised in the Midwest during the 60's, Andy Jacobs is a firm believer in the valuable commodities of loyalty, hard work, tenacity and teamwork.

Graduating from Western International University with a Bachelor of Science in Business, with an emphasis on Productions and Operations Management, he has worked in start-ups, small and medium sized companies.

Combining his schooling with practical life experiences, Andy soon ventured into the entrepreneurial arena. Throughout the past 18 years, he has started and developed four successful ventures, with the assistance of a quality group of coworkers.

Andy views his ventures and business in general as a ripe harvest of mentoring opportunities looking for a place to happen. He uses his businesses as a platform to help coworkers and clients alike, to grow personally and professionally.

The bottom line? People don't come to work for a company; they come to work for a philosophy!

J7 LLC

Sacramento, CA • 916-391-0190 • Andy-Jacobs@J7LLC.com

Andy Jacobs

Golden Handcuffs

How to Lock-In Customer Loyalty With Superior Service!

What if you could wrap up your customers in chains and never let them go? What if you could know for sure that they'd never seek out your competition? What if you could practically guarantee that they would never go out to bid on a project again, but instead just send it to you?

How do you think that would impact your profits? Don't you think it could significantly boost your bottom line? Help you to get more money out of your business?

Well, I've been doing this for more than 18 years. I can tell you that there IS a way to place your customers in Golden Handcuffs by providing them with service and follow up that's so outstanding they don't even think about leaving for a lower price - or if they do, they soon return.

Let me give you seven ways to clamp on the Golden Handcuffs:

ALWAYS SELL SERVICE... NOT PRICE!

In my companies, we've always done things differently, which has allowed us to charge more for our services than our competitors.

In fact, we've consistently charged as much as 30% to 50% higher than some of our competitors. Yet, on a scale of one to ten, with "1" being we don't have enough business and are about to close the doors, and "10" being we absolutely, positively cannot handle any more business, we've consistently operated at a 9 to 9.5.

Why? Because we've NEVER sold on price. Only and always on service.

We only want clients who understand and appreciate the difference in doing business with an "Industry Leader" instead of a "Low Price Leader."

Our companies are different. When our workers walk in the door of a client's office, they have clean uniforms on. They look sharp. They care about their appearance and the appearance of their equipment. They drive clean trucks. They exhibit personal pride in every area of their work.

That's different in today's business world. It's enough of a difference to set us apart from our competition. So when we go in to sell, we never sell on price. We focus on the service aspect of our business. We talk about how we'll meet their needs and demands and how we'll solve their problems. We emphasize that we do not focus on problems and blame shifting, rather, solutions.

MEETING THEIR DEMANDS: EXCEEDING EXPECTATIONS

People want answers yesterday, so we place great emphasis on making sure our response time is as it should be. I call clients back in a timely manner and get thanked for it, as if I'm not supposed to do that.

Our tagline for Cimarron is "Anticipating Your Needs." We think and plan ahead with our business "crystal ball." If it's at all possible, we will do whatever our clients want us to do. One of our accounts, a large furniture dealership, has their own installation crew and usually performs their own work. Because of our willingness to do "whatever" coupled with outside the box thinking, as captain of our ship, they've nicknamed me "Can do Andrew."

Over the years, we've always tried to be not just receptive to what our customers tell us, but also responsive. A key point to note is there is a vast difference between the two. To listen and not respond is the same as not listening at all. Taking action in response to a customer's request is one key to success and building trust and loyalty. Since we are a proactive company, we consistently ask our clients, "How can we better serve you?"

See page 10 for exclusive reader-only FREE offers!

This attitude and question has helped us greatly to diversify. We've blossomed from one company into four. We are always searching for cutting edge ideas, services and concepts we can employ, which will continue to separate ourselves from the competition.

Generally speaking, there are two ways of providing installation labor in the furniture industry. First, you can supply your labor to a dealership that sells furniture and doesn't have their own crew, or one who may need additional installers during flush times.

Secondly, you can supply your labor services to an end user. These are companies who need assistance with rearranging their office space and who do not have the capability.

Regardless of the scenario, when it comes to service, going above and beyond is the ticket to success. Remember, in today's society, mediocrity is the norm. If you go a shade above that, people will think you are outstanding. If you truly excel, you will have more referral work than you can handle, which leads me to the next point.

If you properly and precisely execute the first business opportunity your client presents you with, you will gain their confidence and trust. This, in turn, will render many more discussions on how you can be of future service to them.

When people trust you with one venue, they're definitely open to you presenting them with others. This is your opportunity to diversify and help to lock in their loyalty and business by providing them with "One Stop Shopping."

SOLVING PROBLEMS

Remember, once you secure your client's trust and become the go to guy, you now become their problem solver.

In today's fast paced business world, there is barely time to accomplish the daily tasks of processing paperwork, returning phone calls, answering e-mails and planning for the next day. The last thing your client needs is an unexpected delay due to a problem which has arisen.

When an issue arises which falls into your arena of service, don't be surprised when the phone rings and your client is on the other end. They are turning to you for knowledge, advice and a solution.

It is late on a Friday morning and you are heading out for that long awaited afternoon golf outing. You receive a frantic phone call from your client stating that one of their water pipes burst and the furniture needs to be moved out of the way in order to access the wall. What will you do? Will you drop what you are doing and start to coordinate your resources in order to promptly assist your customer? Or, will you tell your customer you are tied up for the afternoon, but will address it first thing the next morning and have a crew out to assist with the furniture removal?

If you answered the latter, you have just opened the door of opportunity for your competitor! To your customer, that crisis is now the most important issue in their life. They are looking for support, assistance and answers. What they really want to hear is that you will line up the resources necessary ASAP and make it happen. Opportunity is knocking! You then offer your client moving cartons and assistance in packing. You say you will contact your phone and data technician to remove the appropriate wiring from the furniture. This list can go on and on.

Help your customer to solve their issues at hand. It is one of the quickest ways to develop camaraderie and loyalty to your organization.

ATTENTION TO DETAIL

When it comes to servicing your clients, it's all about image.

In most industries and sectors of business, the products and services we receive are relatively the same. What is it then that separates car manufacturers, allowing one to charge $80,000 for a vehicle while the other one charges only $35,000 for something virtually similar?

It is that attention to detail. The stitching in the leather is matching and precise. The doors align perfectly. The dashboard trim fits just right. All of these and more.

This philosophy starts at the top and permeates itself down through the organization. When people come to work for your organization, they should immediately realize that they have come to work for a philosophy, not a paycheck.

Your customers should sense your commitment to excellence through the interaction with your office and field personnel, not just you.

It is taking the time to remove and rethread that cross threaded screw. It is taking the time to wipe out the ash tray when detailing an automobile. The obscure things your customer may not see, but you know about. Will you choose to do the right thing when it appears that nobody is looking or will ever find out?

In the same way, it is our responsibility to train and educate our personnel on details. Teaching them to be efficient and thorough is far more productive than taking short cuts. Too often in business, we take time to go back and fix a mistake instead of doing the job properly the first time.

We always preached that good was the enemy of great. A good job was not acceptable. We pushed ourselves so that we could hear the customer tell us that we did an awesome, great or tremendous job. Was it for our ego? No, but rather to be a reflection of the quality of work we owed our customer for the financial remuneration we were receiving.

ENGAGE YOUR PEOPLE

The little things in life can make a significant difference. And making our coworkers part of the team has produced such a difference, along with a synergistic effect.

As I mentioned before, we took the time to train our personnel not only on technical issues, but also on how to handle professional and personal matters. A long time ago, we realized that the statement "Knowledge is Power" was missing something. The reality we discovered was that "Knowledge applied is Power".

Knowledge alone is synonymous to having a race car without a gas pedal. Until you step on the gas, you are not going to go anywhere. However, the harder you press the pedal, the faster the car will go. Along the same vein of thinking, the more you apply the knowledge, the greater your results.

Part of this was realizing that operating a business and having coworkers is a two way street. We were always teaching and giving knowledge in order to be on the cutting edge.

Engaging our coworkers in company meetings and maintaining open door policies has given our personnel a level of comfort to share ideas no matter how crazy they may sound. Not all ideas received are used, but rather tested for feasibility and then adopted if they bear merit.

The ideas are not what we found important, but rather the desire for our people to be part of something good and a wish to make it better.

FOLLOW UP

How many times have each of us purchased a product or service, had a problem, made a phone call and never heard back? Tragically, in today's business environment follow up is almost non existent. No service after the sale.

In most businesses today, it is all about the bottom line and doing whatever it takes to increase the profit. Over the years it has dawned upon me that there is a vast difference between a company being profit oriented and profit motivated.

We all know that we are in business to make money and in fact need to make a profit; otherwise we will not be around for long. A company that is profit oriented realizes this and incorporates it into their philosophy. On the other hand, a company that is profit motivated is willing to take short cuts, compromise their integrity and do whatever is in their best interest to increase sales and boost profits.

Proper follow up, in reality, can be a great resource to assist you in streamlining and tailoring your business to meet your customers' needs. That simple phone call can provide you with a wealth of information on what you are doing right, as well as on the things you are doing wrong, thus providing you with the information you need to adjust your business gyroscope and make the appropriate changes.

To be on the cutting edge, you need to be proactive. Pick up the phone and ask your clients how you are doing. Take the time to drop your clients a hand written thank you note from time to time. The benefits you will reap from this will far exceed your expectations.

Learn not to leave loose ends. If you have a problem with your service or product, keep the customers abreast of your plans to bring resolution to that issue. I would venture to say that your customers are just like you and me. They know problems will arise occasionally and all they want is to be assured that you are aware of them and working on a solution. It's that simple. We don't need to make rocket science out of Tinkertoys! Do what you say you are going to do.

Aside from some of the standard follow up practices like phone calls, e-mails, etc., we try to think outside the box and be a "novelty." This thought process alone has helped us to differentiate ourselves from the competition.

See page 10 for exclusive reader-only FREE offers!

OUR PHILOSOPHY OF SERVICE

We don't focus on how much cheaper we are than other companies. We don't waste energy sharpening our pencils to get business. Instead, we determine how much time, money and stress we can save our clients in the long run and then present it to them. We outline how much better and more enjoyable we'll make their lives. We align ourselves with them as an ally in order to conquer their arduous task at hand.

Our ideal clients respond to this type of information. It closes more sales for us than any price-driven sales model ever could. We strictly sell service and not price.

We know our niche and focus all of our resources and efforts on it to become the absolute best service provider in our field.

Everything we do has to be a win-win and mutually beneficial for all parties involved. If it's not, we go back to the drawing board and look at it again from a different vantage point, figure out what we need to do to make the changes and finally implement them.

To assist me in this mindset, when entering into a contract, I always ask myself if what I am doing is in the best interest of our client as well as our organization. If the answer is no, I need to assess and reevaluate my plans.

A good benchmark that I have implemented for myself to keep me on the straight and true is the concept of "justification." If I am looking at a contract that appears to be weighted in our favor and find myself "justifying" our position, then I know that I am wrong. If I truly believed in my proposal, then why would I be trying to convince myself that I deserved the terms of this contract? If you follow this principle, then you will never sear your conscience and in turn can truly allow your conscience to be your guide.

"How does this relate to service?" you may be asking. Our belief is that if our customers know where we stand on integrity, they will know that when it comes to quality service and providing nothing but the best, they are guaranteed to receive it.

When it comes to our philosophy on pricing, we believe that if the customer trusts you and knows that they are going to receive paramount service, bar none, then the pricing issue will take care of itself.

If ever questioned on price, our standard answer to a new client is that we predicate our rates on the following three premises:

- We require proper finances to train and uniform our personnel, maintain our vehicles / equipment properly and provide quality service

- We provide a wage and benefit package which will allow our coworkers to maintain a reasonable lifestyle

- We need to have sufficient profits that will enable us to operate our business properly and be here in the years to come to serve them

When pricing is presented in this manner, people can relate to it. The above are what all of us desire, so it makes sense to them.

Whatever philosophy and mindset you choose for your business, stick to it. You don't need to be a jack of all trades; you can choose to be a master of one and above all "The Master" of one.

✱✱✱✱✱✱✱✱✱✱✱✱

If your service and follow up dwarf what the competition has to offer, you can rest assured that you will be able to place the Golden Handcuffs firmly on your customers' wrists. With the outstanding service and one stop shopping you provide, they won't need or desire to go elsewhere.

Give your customers what they need, when and how they want it. In so doing, it will be a win for all parties involved and you will profit as they'll come back again and again - and again.

See page 10 for exclusive reader-only FREE offers!

FREE!
Continue Your Learning And
Business-Building Online:
www.MDMSbonus.com

CHAPTER FIFTEEN

Legendary Branding

How to Make Magic Through Every Touch with a Customer or Prospect!

Ben Mack

Speaker & Brand Strategist

Ben Mack (Troy, NY) is a sales and marketing expert and a career ad-man-former Senior Vice President BBDO, J. Walter Thompson Planning Director, Memeticist for WONGDOODY and winner of the American Marketing Association"s Edison Award and Effie Award.

He's the author of *Think Two Products Ahead* (John Wiley & Sons, 2007), which teaches readers how to use the same techniques and technologies as the big players-but without all the cost. Ben Mack discloses insider shortcuts for power positioning, framing a product properly, connecting with the consumer, and prioritizing marketing ideas.

"If you aren't thinking two products ahead, you're either leaving money on the table or you're a hustler," says Mack.

"Creating loyalty beyond reason and moving from irreplaceable to irresistible is job #1 for all marketers today. Ben's book will help you get there," says Kevin Roberts, CEO Saatchi & Saatchi Worldwide

Ben speaks internationally from MBA Lectures to Harv Eker's World's Greatest Marketing Seminar, to Speakers' Bureau events on these topics:

- Brand = Your Corporate Culture Code
- Creativity On Demand
- Using Fun for Bigger Profits

Ben Mack
Atlanta, GA • 404-725-2121 • www.thinktwoproductsahead.com

Ben Mack

Legendary Branding

How to Make Magic Through Every Touch with a Customer or Prospect!

Marketing companies may use different words in their branding scheme, with different labels and pictures, but virtually all of them use the same three steps:

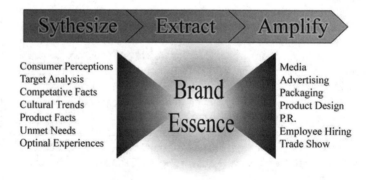

Sythesize > Extract > Amplify

Consumer Perceptions	Media
Target Analysis	Advertising
Competative Facts	Packaging
Cultural Trends	Product Design
Product Facts	P.R.
Unmet Needs	Employee Hiring
Optinal Experiences	Trade Show

Brand Essence

Ideally, a brand essence remains virtually unchanged from one decade to the next. The advertising and packaging of your brand may change, but a true brand essence remains constant. I know I said that earlier, but most brand managers get caught up with the functionality of their products without seeing the bigger picture of their brand essence.

Sergio Zyman uses the term core essence instead of brand

essence. Fine. Same difference. Zyman suggesting understanding how your core essence is relevant now and how it is becoming relevant is the heart of sustainable business...

> "You may think you're innovating, but you're probably just wasting money. Try renovating instead...A recent disaster is the Walkman. While Sony was busy making colorful new versions of personal, portable CD players, Apple was out there redefining portable entertainment. Sony should have introduced iPods, not Apple. So what was the domain of Sony is now Apple's forever."
> Sergio Zyman
> "The Innovation Illusion"
> CMO Magazine, 2/26/06

You're essence is what you're building and reinforcing.

The objective of extraction is to create a platform that leverages the favorable conditions identified during synthesis. This is a battle for a mind and you want to engage on the most advantageous terrain.

> "Military strategists know that most battles are won before the first shot is fired-by the side that determines where, when and how an engagement is fought...Political professionals call the act of defining the terrain of engagement 'framing the debate.'"
> -James Carville & Paul Begala
> Buck Up, Suck Up

In branding, your essence is your terrain. Your essence should be a ground where, if you were challenged, you would likely win.

I argue that once a brand essence is identified, the company should structure itself around delivering that brand essence. A brand essence needs to be more than communication talk points. **A brand essence needs to be a vision to continuously grow into.**

> "A Brahmin is not a Brahmin because he is born a Brahmin, but because his body is an arrow and his soul is a bow and with all his might he is aiming his soul at being Brahmin."
> -Herman Hesse
> Siddhartha

A brand essence is not a brand essence because you state it; a brand essence exists only to the extent your whole organization actively generates this essence.

See page 10 for exclusive reader-only FREE offers!

Making money is why your company exists, but let's put that aside for this exercise. Why do customers give you money? Hannibal Lecter coached, "Read Marcus Aurelius. Of each particular thing ask: what is it in itself?"

For Corona drinking their beer isn't about the flavor or getting a buzz as much as it is a statement of "this is play time."

Most people aren't buying the function of a product, but their associations with the brand or the feelings of the style...they're buying something beyond the function.

You see, there's a functional thing a product or service does and then there's a bigger space with an emotional benefit. **Emotions are the key to loyalty.**

Consistently promising and delivering on an emotion creates loyalty; you desire unreasonable customers, customers willing to pay more than average for a product and not to think about any other source for their satisfaction.

Consistency is the backbone of a longstanding trust. What follows are tools for consistency and continuity of messaging, Legendary Branding.

Brands live in their stories...some of the stories are seeded by commercials and other communications like packaging, websites and answering machine messages. However, there are many, many stories about our products and services that we don't script. Yesterday, when we ordered a Dominos Pizza...those kind of stories.

Why is it people feel more compelled to share negative experiences? I don't know, but for the sake of your brand, please try and keep your customers happy. For my sake, I hope you find these ideas actionable and profitable.

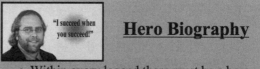

"I succeed when you succeed!"

Hero Biography

- Within every legend there must be a hero
  - A character whose story is told
- Your customer is the hero of your story...your product or service is what facilitates their heroic activities
- In identifying your hero biography, we are locating and defining the core essence of your brand

Did you read that? **Your customer is your story's hero; your product or service is what facilitates their heroic activities.** These words on this page are meaningless unless it helps people make more money.

The greatest honor of writing a business book is having people I have never met take my words seriously and work through these ideas for themselves. The greatest thrill is when they share how it has helped them. Joost van der Leij has profited from these ideas. When he wrote me with suggestions for improvement, I implemented as much as I could, knowing there were other readers with very similar perspectives. If I could make this material more useable to Joost, others would be more likely to replicate his success.

> "Before I received an advance copy of Ben Mack's Think Two Products Ahead, I was a 'successful' direct response practitioner...Nice five figure income. Ever since I implemented these ideas from early January 2006 on, I have been adjusting my forecast upward. Original I had planned for a 50% increase in sales in 2006, but today, March 1st, even **my most conservative forecasts mean doubling revenues in 2006.**
>
> - Google Click Through Rate jumped from 5.1% to 9.1%
> - Subscriptions to my free newsletter increased from 100 to 150 per week to anything between 250 and 350 people each week
> - Sales have gone up 206% month over month
>
> But going beyond the cold figures, I now have a much better understanding of my relationship with my clients, my communication with them and most important the reason why they choose to do business with me. I am happy to say that I now have found a process by which I am enable to do the work I love most ... for the rest of my life. No more uncertainty about the future, for I am assured of more work than I can handle each and every day."
> Joost van der Leij, CEO, TIOUW.com BV
> For more information see http://www.tiouw.com/en/

Who is your hero? Your customer. Your customer is the hero of your story. The person you are fighting to help be successful. Joost is my hero. The tools and techniques in this book facilitated his heroic business growth, Joost did the work and had the fortitude to follow-through and implement these ideas.

Let's look at Clif Bar-made by athletes for athletes. A Clif Bar user is somebody who has such a good time doing out-door physical activities that they need extra energy in the form of an energy bar.

See page 10 for exclusive reader-only FREE offers!

But this person also enjoys great taste. The funky taste of a Power Bar just doesn't work for them, especially that chemical after-taste.

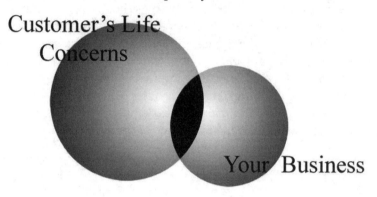

Talk about the stuff that overlaps, but which stuff do you talk about?

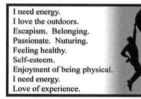 

You want your customer to see themselves in your communications.

Humans are tribal. We look for our kind...the logos and flags that we see as..."That's me."

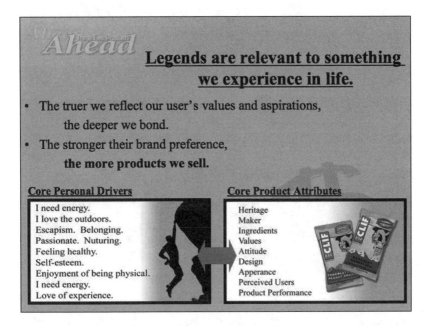

Legends are relevant to something we experience in life.

- The truer we reflect our user's values and aspirations, the deeper we bond.
- The stronger their brand preference, **the more products we sell.**

Core Personal Drivers	Core Product Attributes
I need energy.	Heritage
I love the outdoors.	Maker
Escapism. Belonging.	Ingredients
Passionate. Nuturing.	Values
Feeling healthy.	Attitude
Self-esteem.	Design
Enjoyment of being physical.	Apperance
I need energy.	Perceived Users
Love of experience.	Product Performance

All of our customers are heroes, but we don't always show all our customers.

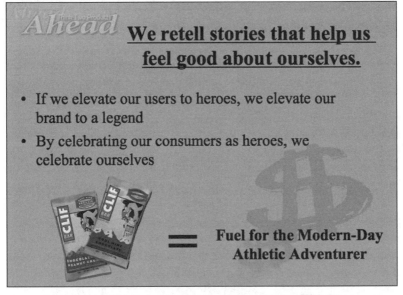

We retell stories that help us feel good about ourselves.

- If we elevate our users to heroes, we elevate our brand to a legend
- By celebrating our consumers as heroes, we celebrate ourselves

= Fuel for the Modern-Day Athletic Adventurer

See page 10 for exclusive reader-only FREE offers!

How do we use this information for consistent communications?

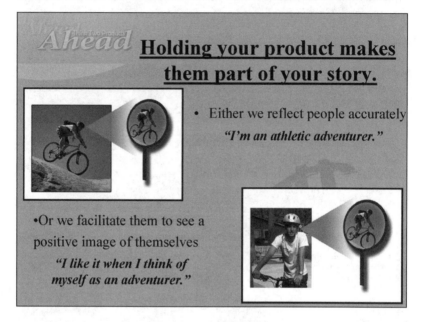

Holding your product makes them part of your story.

- Either we reflect people accurately
  "I'm an athletic adventurer."

- Or we facilitate them to see a positive image of themselves
  "I like it when I think of myself as an adventurer."

After working out this process, Clif Bar was more comfortable thinking of themselves as standing for Mojo than *Fuel For The Modern Day Adventurer*. That's fine. Their ads regularly show an athlete accomplishing

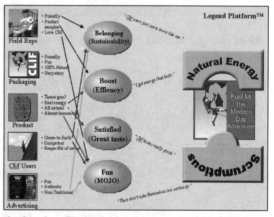

something outrageously kooky (heroic) that requires extraordinary energy (fuel). That's Clif Bar Mojo. Other ads discuss the efficacy of their natural products and how good they taste. That's Clif Bar Mojo.

Clif Bar marketers have a great intuitive sense of what they are communicating because they are a community of their target audience. However, the diagram above allows a team to better understand their options. Every communication, every association with Clif Bar packaging or communications are intended to reinforce at least one of these emotions: belonging, boost, satisfaction or fun.

In addition, we want to position Clif Bar as scrumptious fuel that allows its eater to accomplish heroic feats. If every touch with a Clif bar reinforces these ideas, they are building their brand equity.

Your Legend Platform communicates your brand essence in such a way that:

- Communications have emotional objectives
  - Advertising, packaging and collateral have a unified vision to build
- Teammates know what they are working towards
  - Employees have a tool that teaches and reinforces best-practices by showing a big picture vision of the consumer's experience

---

*This chapter is adapted from **Think Two Products Ahead**, by Ben Mack, (John Wiley & Sons 2007, ISBN: 0-470-05576-6)*

FREE!

**Continue Your Learning And
Business-Building Online:
www.MDMSbonus.com**

CHAPTER SIXTEEN

Make Your Product's Benefits Sparkle

5 Steps to Connect Product Benefits with Prospects' Most Powerful Response-Boosting Emotions

Clayton Makepeace

Direct Response Marketing Consultant and Copywriter

As a working direct response marketing consultant and copywriter since 1971, Clayton Makepeace has produced hundreds of direct mail, Internet and print ad promotions - including many of America's most effective campaigns for investment and health newsletters and books, nutritional supplements and many other products.

Clayton's sales copy and marketing guidance have generated as many as 2 million new subscribers for a single publisher in just 36 months ... produced annual revenue and profit growth of up to 3,700% for his investment and health newsletter and nutritional supplement clients and, all-told, have sold well over $1 billion-worth of products.

Clayton's marketing agency, Response Ink™, currently produces successful customer acquisition and house file promotions for many of the most successful marketers in the investment and health industries.

In June 2005, Clayton founded The Profit Center™ and his weekly marketing e-newsletter, The Total Package™ to share his proven response-boosting techniques with copywriters, business owners and marketing professionals.

In October 2005, Clayton Makepeace was named The American Writers and Artists Institute "Copywriter of the Year."

Bob Bly, author of The Complete Idiot's Guide to Direct Marketing and The Copywriters Handbook says "Clayton Makepeace is the real deal. Not only is he one of the three best copywriters in the industry, he may be the single most successful copywriter in the world."

The Profit Center™

Jupiter, FL • 1-800-827-0940 • www.MakepeaceTotalPackage.com

Clayton Makepeace

Make Your Product's Benefits Sparkle

5 Steps to Connect Product Benefits with Prospects' Most Powerful Response-Boosting Emotions

Are "Faux Benefits" killing your products sales copy?

The other day, I had the dubious pleasure of reviewing copy submitted by a new group of copywriters (copy cubs) - each of whom completed courses on copywriting ... and I believe each has the innate talent to (eventually) become a great copywriter.

Each copy cub was asked to write benefit-oriented headlines for a series of natural supplement products.

The first headline jumped up and shouted...

GET OFF THE HORMONE ROLLER COASTER!

"Well," I said to myself, "THAT certainly stinks!" And so I turned to the next one ...

FLUSH DEADLY TOXINS OUT OF YOUR COLON!

"Whoo boy," I said out loud, "I should be getting combat pay for this!"

See, not a single one of those "benefit-based" headlines contains a single real benefit! Instead, each contains a "Faux Benefit" - a product feature masquerading as a benefit!

Apply my patented "forehead slap" test to each of those headlines and you'll see what I mean.

- Have you ever been awakened in the middle of the night... sat bolt upright in bed ... slapped yourself on the forehead and exclaimed, "Holy Moley - I gotta get off of the hormone roller coaster?"

- And when was the last time you were jarred out of a deep sleep exclaiming "I gotta flush some deadly toxins out of my colon!"

Have you ever found yourself feeling eager to PAY for a product that would do any of those things for you?

Of course not. Our "hormone balancing" prospects want to stop having hot flashes and mood swings and stop losing their libidos.

And frankly, while "flushing toxins out of my colon" is nowhere near the top of my personal "to do" list, I WOULD prefer not to be constipated, or plagued with uncontrollable diarrhea, or die from colon cancer.

The Faux Benefits heralded in these headlines are product features that deliver benefits. They are not, in themselves, real benefits that anybody craves or wants to *pay for*.

My beloved copy cubs failed to drill down to the real benefit each product provides - the tangible, real value that prospects are willing to pay for.

This is a cardinal and common sin even among the most seasoned copywriters, business owners and marketing execs.

Here's another: Failing to fully explore the benefits that each benefit provides. In short, squeezing every feature until you've explored every benefit ... and then squeezing every benefit for the secondary benefits IT provides.

BENEFITS 101

Let's start with four basic facts...

1. **Every product has features:** Features are merely objective facts about a product (or the company behind it). Features include size, shape and weight, number of pages, frequency of publication, construction, color options and more.

2. **Fortunately, most features are there for a darned good reason:** Prospects don't want features. They want you to change their lives for the better.

See page 10 for exclusive reader-only FREE offers!

Product features are merely the means to that end. Beyond that, features are a yawn because they're about the product; not about the prospect. Including features in sales copy can help demonstrate how your product delivers a benefit.

The good news is, just about every product feature is there to provide a benefit that your prospect IS willing to pay for.

3.   There are more benefits associated with each product feature than are dreamt of by most copywriters: Benefits are like bunny rabbits: Give them a little time and they'll begin multiplying.

The secret to super responsive sales copy is to identify each and every benefit a product provides - and then to look at each benefit and ask, "What does THAT do for me? What additional benefits does that benefit provide?"

4.   Your prospect has strong feelings about every dimensionalized benefit you present: Connecting each fully dimensionalized product benefit with a strong emotion that your prospect already has about the benefit makes sales copy irresistible.

BENEFITS THAT SING AND SOAR
– IN FIVE SIMPLE STEPS

Here's a little exercise to help you drill down to the benefits prospects are willing to pay for. By the time you're through, you will have a comprehensive "features/benefits/dominant emotion" inventory you can refer to as you write your product sales copy.

To begin, create a spreadsheet with these headings:

Feature	Why?	Benefits	Dimensionalize	Dominant Emotions	Rank

STEP #1:
CREATE A COMPREHENSIVE
FEATURES INVENTORY

Features are the fathers of each benefit your product provides. And if every product benefit has its roots in a product feature, identifying and fully understanding each feature is essential to identifying all the benefits your product provides.

So start by listing all the key facts about 1) the business and 2) the product or service you're promoting.

Answer the following questions about the company and the spokesperson behind the product in the first column of your table:

A. "What are your qualifications?" What degrees or certifications have you earned in your field of endeavor? From which institutions? What associations are you a member of? How many years have you provided this product or service?

How many customers (patients, clients, etc.) have you served? Are you the largest or oldest in your area of expertise? What specialties do you offer that your competitors don't?

B. "What resources do you use to produce a superior product or service?" How many employees are working on the prospect's behalf? What unique or proprietary tools do you use to produce the desired result?

How many customer service reps are available to make ordering comfortable and easy? How many service technicians are standing by should the product need service or the prospect need support?

C. "How is your location a factor?" Are you closer to your prospects than the competition? Is your office close to a major intersection or freeway off-ramp? Do you offer plenty of free parking?

Or, if you're a national company, how does your location help you produce a superior product? Are you offering an investment product that's produced on Wall Street, for example?

D. "What's your reaction time?" Are appointments readily available? Do you perform your service faster than your competition? If I order this product, how fast will I get it?

E. Inventory: How many different products do you have available? How does that compare to what your competitors offer?

PRODUCT OR SERVICE FEATURES

Now, it's time to really start digging - with answers about the product or service you're offering:

A. Purpose: What, *exactly*, does your product or service do? If it accomplishes several things - list everything you can think of!

B. Physical dimensions: How does your product compare to competing products? Is it smaller? Bigger? Lighter? Stronger?

If it's a published product for instance, how many pages are in the book? Is the page or type size larger that what the prospect may be used to? If it is a periodical, is it published more frequently?

C. Performance metrics: How quickly can your product be delivered, installed and/or begin producing results? How fast does your product complete the desired task? How thoroughly does it do its job? How long does it last? How do your product's performance metrics compare to similar products offered by your competitors?

D. Credibility: What have customers, subscribers, peers and others said about your product or service? What guarantees and/or warranties come with it? How do they compare to what the competition offers?

E. Available options: What choices does your product offer to prospects? What colors or sizes does it come in? How do your terms make ordering the best fit possible for customers? Is it customizable in any way? How do these choices make your product superior to the competition?

F. Timeliness: How quickly can your product be delivered and/or installed? How does this compare with the competition?

G. Pricing: What are your prices? How do they compare to the competition? Do you deliver more for the money? Or does your product's quality demand a higher price?

These are just a few idea-starters - please do not stop here!

Use this opportunity to think through every step of the process that your prospects experience when shopping for, buying and using your product or service.

STEP #2:
ATTACH A "WHY" TO EACH FEATURE

The next step is to figure out why these features are included in the product or service, and then to turn those reasons into tangible benefits that will bring value to the customer's life.

So now, in the "WHY?" column next to each feature, enter the benefits each feature provides.

Example: If you're selling a high quality drill bit, your entry might look like this:

Feature: Constructed of carbon steel.

Why: Never wears out.

Or, if you're writing for a book on health, you might write ...

Feature: Specific prescription for each age group on each supplement recommended.

Why: To eliminate reader confusion.

Attach as many "whys" to each feature as you can.

My guess is that as you review your completed list, you'll be getting pretty excited. Your brain is already beginning to take the next step - visualizing how these features improve your customers' lives!

STEP #3:
TURN FEATURES INTO BENEFITS

The simple act of completing Steps #1 and #2 above could easily multiply your sales and profits by tens of thousands of dollars - merely by shifting the spotlight off the advertiser and his product or service and on to why the features are important to the customer.

But still, we've focused entirely on the product or service. Now, we're going to bring your prospect into the picture - and answer the question, *"What's in it for me? How does each of these features - these facts about the business and product or service - directly connect with and improve my life?"*

Think about how each feature and "Reason Why" benefits your customer, and list every possible way each one of them brings value to your prospect's life.

We're going to ask the one question that's constantly at the forefront of your customer's mind: *"What's in it for me?"*

And we're going to answer by listing the problems your product or service solves ... the desires it fulfills ... and the future disasters it will help your customers avoid.

See page 10 for exclusive reader-only FREE offers!

Be sure to think about immediate benefits as well as those the customer will experience later on.

If you're selling one-hour oil changes for example, you can save your customer oodles of time right now, today. But you also make it easy for him to properly maintain the family chariot, thereby helping him avoid an inconvenient or even dangerous breakdown and costly repairs later on.

Write each benefit as a "you" statement - as if you're talking face-to-face with your prospective customer, patient or client.

Then, go back over your list of benefits ... look at each one ... and ask yourself, "What additional benefits does this benefit bring to my life?" Keep drilling down until you hit the Mother Lode - the benefits that mean the most and bring the most value to prospects' lives.

STEP #4:
DIMENSIONALIZE EACH BENEFIT

When you "dimensionalize" a benefit, you give it added dimension by painting word pictures of all the ways the prospect will enjoy that benefit. You compare that benefit with those offered by others. You add specifics that demonstrate all the ways the benefit will enrich the prospect's life.

When finished, your list may look something like this, for example:

Feature: Constructed of carbon steel.

Why: Never wears out.

Benefit: The last drill bit you'll ever buy.

Dimensionalized Benefit: You can save up to $75 a year in broken drill bits ... hours of unnecessary trips to the hardware store ... and hundreds of dollars in lost income!

Or, if you're writing for a book on health, your list might look something like this...

Feature: Specific prescription for each age group on each supplement recommended.

Why: To eliminate reader confusion.

Dimensionalize: You'll always know precisely what you should be taking ... how much you should be taking ... and even when to take it.

STEP #5:
CONNECT EACH DIMENSIONALIZED BENEFIT WITH A DOMINANT RESIDENT EMOTION

Connecting with your prospects' most dominant resident emotions gives you a big edge over writers who focus only on the benefits a product provides.

You can be sure that every customer or prospect you will ever talk to shares common fears, frustrations and desires ...

Allow me to demonstrate by using the example of the health book above ...

Feature: Specific prescription for each age group on each supplement recommended.

Why: To eliminate reader confusion.

Dimensionalize: You'll always know precisely what you should be taking ... how much you should be taking ... and even when to take it.

Dominant Resident Emotion: You'll feel completely confident and independent ... Not reliant on your children, friends or a medical provider for assistance ... Able to sleep better at night knowing you're not a burden on your family ... At peace because you'll live a long, healthy life with plenty of quality time to spend with your precious grandchildren.

The point is simply to identify how your prospect is likely to feel about each of the dimensionalized benefits on your list.

Do NOT stop at listing just one emotion per benefit. Think about how the prospect feels about the lack of this benefit in his or her life now. And about how the prospect will feel as he or she is enjoying that benefit. And about how they'll feel as others see them doing things better ... being healthier ... richer ... happier.

Then, USE your list to make sure you press every possible hot button as you begin writing your copy - and please, for mercy's sake - to get real, dimensionalized, emotionalized BENEFITS into your headline and lead copy!

See page 10 for exclusive reader-only FREE offers!

FREE!

**Continue Your Learning And
Business-Building Online:
www.MDMSbonus.com**

CHAPTER SEVENTEEN

Strategic Marketing Multipliers

How to Create Windfall Business Profits With The Power of Leverage!

JP Maroney

Business Growth Strategist, Author, Speaker & Serial Entrepreneur

Famous for his uncanny ability to help business owners remove limitations to their revenue growth and build multi-million dollar businesses, JP Maroney's clients call him "the man with the Million-Dollar Midas Touch" ... and *Entrepreneur Magazine* calls his methods "wildly generous."

A veteran business builder and serial entrepreneur, JP has...
- Founded 7 companies
- Bought five others
- And played "Dealmaker" in countless ventures

As Founder and Chairman of Marocom Group, the international consulting, publishing and training firm specializing in strategic business growth and development – JP lives and breathes profitable growth every day.

In the words of his clients, JP's business consultations are worth "tens of millions" to their businesses.

JP is a business growth strategist, best-selling author and award-winning speaker. He's Executive Producer and Host of "People Builders," a video-based continuous performance improvement system.

A frequent keynote speaker and seminar leader, JP teaches proven principles, ideas and strategies that have been hammered out on the anvil of experience.

JP is the author or co-author of more than 30 books, audio training programs, and video learning systems.

MAROCOM, LLC
Tyler, Texas • 1-800-304-5758 • www.JPMaroney.com

JP Maroney

Strategic Marketing Multipliers
How to Create Windfall Business Profits With The Power of Leverage!

Since you are reading this, you are presumably someone who has a business that can benefit from either...

- More customers
- More revenue
- More profits
- Or all of the above...

I'm willing to bet you've heard the phrase:

"IT'S NOT WHAT YOU KNOW... IT'S WHO YOU KNOW"

If you don't have influential business contacts, you are literally short circuiting your opportunity for sustained business growth and success. However... if you know who to call, when to call, and why (or why not) to call, you've got yourself:

An Outstanding Opportunity To Leverage Your Ideas, Talents, and Resources for Extraordinary Success.

The secret to rapid and lasting business success is in creating partnerships and strategic alliances... also known as Joint Ventures.

However, you may be wondering...

"ARE JOINT VENTURES THE RIGHT WAY TO GROW MY BUSINESS?"

Maybe you're a business owner. You have a thriving business, but you're looking for new ways to make it grow. You want to take your business to the next level.

Maybe you're an idea guy. You have scores of great business ideas, but lack the resources to fund them.

Maybe you have a special talent... like copywriting, computer programming or graphic design... and all you need is a project where you can put your expertise to use.

Maybe you have money, but you're short on time. You need other people's talents and time to put your money to work.

Maybe you have a big list of hungry buyers... and you need a steady stream of great products and services to offer them.

Maybe you have no list, product or money... but you have the ambition to put list owners and product creators together - you want to become one of the elite JV Dealmakers who brokers "deals" between two or more businesses.

No matter what it is you need... joint ventures can realistically and quickly solve your challenge. I'm really talking about...

THE ULTIMATE LEVERAGE

Joint ventures deliver the power to leverage the resources and assets of other people and businesses. Once you understand these principles, you'll never look at your contacts and relationships the same way again.

Truth is, no matter what you call them... Joint Ventures, Strategic Alliances, Endorsements, Parasite Marketing, Host-Beneficiary Relationships, and Partners are really about "LEVERAGE."

They're all about leveraging...

OPL = Other People's Lists
OPC = Other People's Credibility
OPM = Other People's Money
OPR = Other People's Relationships
OPP = Other People's Products
OPT = Other People's Time
OPE = Other People's Expertise

See page 10 for exclusive reader-only FREE offers!

And, the reality is...

ALL IT TAKES IS ONE

What if right now you knew you were only one contact away from a Joint Venture or Strategic Partnership that would drastically improve your businesses' bottom line? One contact that could create a flood of new sales leads for your business? A flood of hungry buyers?

How would that change your outlook?

Just one strategic alliance, business partnership, or joint venture can double, triple, or quadruple your profit margin.

After you've tasted your first JV success... once you see how easy and lucrative JVs can be... you'll be rabid for more. There's simply no faster way to achieve the wealth and success you desire.

ALLIANCES MAKE THE WORLD GO 'ROUND

Consider these famous and wildly successful business alliances:

- Bill Gates and Paul Allen
- Mark Victor Hansen and Jack Canfield
- Rich DeVoss and Jay Van Andel
- Andrew Carnegie and Napolean Hill
- Al Ries and Jack Trout

There's no end to the long list of Joint Ventures that have literally changed the world. Almost every single individual who has achieved extraordinary success has achieved it because of a Joint Venture of some kind.

Work 50% less and get 150% more results by doing what the JV experts do - leveraging off other people's efforts, sitting back and reaping all the rewards.

Many of the world's most successful people got started leveraging off of someone else. They used that person's capital, expertise, time or customer list to propel their own business forward.

They took advantage of an existing situation and they capitalized on it to make themselves a success.

Look at H. Ross Perot, Michael Dell, Bill Gates, and Tony

Robbins. Each one of these mega-success stories literally climbed on the backs of someone else to get them where they are today.

SCREW THE ECONOMY... MAKE MONEY YEAR IN AND YEAR OUT!

It doesn't matter if the economy is in a downward spiral. It doesn't matter what the political climate is like. Even in wartime, savvy marketers go to work, riding on their alliances all the way to the bank!

And, why not? There's no shame in riding someone else's coattails, not spending a cent of your own money, or simply coming up with an idea and letting someone else do all the work.

Multiply Your Marketing!

One of the easiest to understand, and simplest ways to exploit the concept of joint-ventures, is to use it as a way to "Multiply Your Marketing." You utilize the customer and prospect lists of other marketers to get your product sales message out quickly to more potential buyers, without spending a fortune of your own money on advertising and marketing.

Most commonly, marketer A will have a list of customers who have purchased a product and another marketer B will have a new product. Marketer A promotes marketer B's product to his customer list in exchange for a commission.

Their combined forces produce profits that neither of them would have enjoyed had they not done a joint venture together.

HOW TO FIND PARTNERS

When looking for joint venture partners, it is always better to first turn to people with whom you have some business relationship. Someone who has bought from you or someone who you have bought from will always be better prospects for joint ventures than people who are "cold" strangers.

It's called "NEER: Naturally Existing Economic Relationships."

Think carefully! Who have you bought from or sold to that has a customer list of the same types of people who might be buyers for your product or service?

See page 10 for exclusive reader-only FREE offers!

Approaching existing relationships will always be easier, and more profitable than total strangers. You're much more likely to do these deals with people who are acquainted with you than with someone who has never heard of you.

If someone has never heard of you or your product, there is some instant, built-in skepticism that you have to work hard to overcome. This is lessened when you joint venture with someone you know.

HOW TO APPROACH PARTNERS

There are numerous ways you can approach prospective joint venture partners. You can approach them in person, by mail, by phone, by email, or by fax.

If you first approach people you already have a relationship with, this will be fairly easy. It's quite natural to pick up the phone and call a "buddy" with the idea of "doing a deal."

It's important to develop the right mindset. Have confidence. Prospects can sense whether your contact is important or not.

You have to revere yourself and believe that this is a valuable business proposition. If you're thinking, "I'm new, I'm not worthy, I don't know if this is gonna work," it may sabotage your success.

This truly is a valuable business deal that you're offering your joint venture partner. It's a win/win deal that serves the customers, your joint venture partner, and yourself. Treat it as such.

Take note of this... Avoid using "blind emails" to pitch joint venture deals. Sure, they're easy and FREE.

One last note: You can also get "JV Partner Prospects" to come to you. For example, I have set up a special website at www.JVwithJP.com specifically for the purpose of allowing people to "pitch their ideas" to me. You can do the same. In fact, one of my co-authors on this project has already "adapted" this idea.

PRESENTING YOUR IDEA

As soon as you make contact with your prospective joint venture partner, give them a short pitch about the joint venture idea. Tell them what's in it for them. Be organized. Speak authoritatively.

Write the selling points out on a piece of paper that you can refer to as you're on the phone, and take notes of what they're saying. You can refer back to these later in follow-up calls and written communications.

If you're talking to the decision maker and they've never done a joint venture before, you're going to have to educate them on the benefits.

You need to stress that doing this joint venture creates almost FREE money for them, that it is easy for them to do (because you'll do most of the work setting it up), and that it won't take money away from what they're doing.

Show them how they can make money. Paint the scenario vividly of what it would be like for them to make money, fairly easily, by doing a joint venture with you.

Eliminate as much of the risk as possible. The less your prospective joint venture partner has to risk in doing a deal with you, the more likely they are to say yes to your pitch.

PROTECTING YOUR IDEA

If you're worried about protecting your idea, then you can protect yourself with a Non-disclosure agreement (NDA). Basically, an NDA binds anybody who signs it from disclosing certain secrets related to the joint venture deal.

The NDA is used to communicate to your joint venture partner that what the joint venture you're putting together is a valuable, exclusive technique that not everyone knows. This communicates to them that this is valuable.

The NDA is to be used with partners who haven't done joint ventures before or who don't really know how joint ventures work. If you're proposing a joint venture to a seasoned marketer, don't bother with an NDA. They already know how joint ventures work and have likely done many of them before.

HOW TO PUT THE DEAL TOGETHER

Depending on the size of the deal, and who you're dealing with, you will want to have some sort of agreement in place. It could be a handshake, a simple letter of agreement or a more detailed formal legal document.

The primary purpose of a written agreement is to make sure everyone is "on the same page" regarding the terms of the joint venture. This is not so much so you can pursue it legally as much as it is to simply avoid misunderstandings.

Your agreement should include details about the time length of the joint venture, who does what, any financial arrangements and how the agreement will be terminated.

See page 10 for exclusive reader-only FREE offers!

SIX JOINT VENTURE EXAMPLES YOU CAN MODEL

Multiple-Author Books: On six separate occasions, including the book your currently reading, I have pulled together from 11 to 19 other authors, speakers, consultants and specialized experts for multiple-author books. Each person contributes a chapter on the given, overall topic of the book.

Cooperative Information Products: You team up with one or more experts who compliment your expertise. Together, you create an information Product. It could be an audio series. It could be video training. It could be a series of special reports or teleseminars.

Business Partnerships: At times, the best way to leverage the talents, resources, and knowledge of two or more people is to form a company where each individual shares in the risks and rewards of the business. I've been involved in start-ups using this model. I've brought partners into an existing business that I started. And, I've "bought in" to existing businesses started by other entrepreneurs. Sometimes my company and another company form a third entity to achieve a business goal. Some have worked handsomely, some have flopped, and some were nerve-racking.

Endorsement Marketing: This is one of the most common "JV's" because it's fairly easy to understand and implement. Essentially, an entrepreneur with a list of customers, clients and prospects sends a sales piece "endorsing" the product or service of another entrepreneur. I've used this method to sell my products and services to members of large trade organizations, customers of other companies, and clients of other professionals. I've "brokered" or set up similar deals for my clients where my client's product or service was promoted to another company's list.

Cooperative Events: Event marketing is a great way to reach prospects and clients. But, it can be expensive and time consuming to put on a large event. Instead of taking it on by yourself, you can team up with other entrepreneurs, companies or professionals so that each person shares the expense, labor demands and marketing resources. Example: I helped one of my clients mastermind a "community service event" where he pulled together several "complimentary" businesses to help with the promotion, prizes and other event details. It worked out nicely, with each "partner" in the deal receiving way more exposure than they could have on their own.

Reciprocal Cross-Promotion: I've set up deals between my clients and complimentary businesses where they each "trade" gift certificate or coupon offers and promote it to their respective clients, customers and prospects. In some cases, we inserted one offer in my client's newsletter. In other cases, we passed out materials through a drive-thru. No money ever changes hands. Yet, each company benefits from the expanded exposure to new prospective buyers.

TAKING THE FIRST STEP...

The next step is to take "the first step." It's one thing to know about joint ventures. It's another thing to do it.

Here are some action steps:

1. Get a FREE copy of "The JV Report" co-authored by me and one of my partners, Marc Goldman. You can find it here: http://www.jpmaroney.com/jvreport

2. Review your rolodex for entrepreneurs or businesses you already have a relationship with that are complimentary but non-competitive to your business.

3. Brainstorm the ideal joint-venture between your two companies. Would it be a cross-promotion? An endorsement deal? Formation of a third business? Think about it.

4. Create a plan to approach at least one joint venture prospect each week for the next ten to twelve weeks - until you've secured at least one "joint venture" deal.

5. Don't worry or quit if your first attempts fail. As with any "new thing," it's natural to have limited or little success in the beginning. Just persist and you will get better at it. You'll become more skilled at explaining the concept.

6. Repeat the process. One of the biggest mistakes I see entrepreneurs make is having a single success with this type of marketing strategy… **and then NEVER doing it again.** Joint ventures can and will provide you with increased leads, sales and profits for many years if you'll just keep repeating the process.

See page 10 for exclusive reader-only FREE offers!

FREE!
Continue Your Learning And
Business-Building Online:
www.MDMSbonus.com

CHAPTER EIGHTEEN

Monkey Bar Marketing

The Fundamentals of Fun and the Art of Playing

Jason "Profit" Moffatt

Internet Marketer & Copywriter

Jason Moffatt is a new-school niche marketer and creative copywriter that was crowned the 2005 "Underachiever Of The Year" by Ed Dale and Frank Kern. Using his underground skills as a Street Smart Private Investigator, Jason deeply understands how to dig into the minds of his prospects and customers like few other copywriters in the world.

Delicately balancing controversial wordplay with an entertaining sales message has proven to be the perfect mixture for Profit Moffatt. If you are looking for buck-wild business strategies and insanely creative marketing angles, here's your guy.

Jason credits his marketing success to the fact that he's always having fun and constantly wants to get a reaction out of people. He genuinely enjoys creating niche empires while brainstorming off-the-wall strategies for starting viral trends.

Experienced as a door-to-door salesman, street magician, cab driver, tour guide, radio show host, political activist, private eye, and business entrepreneur, Jason has an unfathomable amount of experience in the real world.

His provocative and unorthodox style of writing has been catching on like wildfire throughout the internet marketing community. While Jason spends 95% of his time writing copy for his own products, he has been known to occasionally work with a limited group of like-minded clients.

Jason "Profit" Moffatt
San Diego, CA • www.ProfitMoffatt.com

Jason "Profit" Moffatt

Monkey Bar Marketing
The Fundamentals of Fun and the Art of Playing

As I begin to write this chapter to you, I'm sitting inside a plush black limo with my Underachiever pals Ed Dale and Frank Kern. We are currently en route to a killer guitar shop in Orlando, Florida, to strum a plethora of six-strings and to screw off like a clan of high school kids. The entire day is devoted to "Guitar Lovers" and we take this business very seriously. Of course I'm referring to "Monkey Business," not the typical suit and tie type of business.

The majority of successful marketers that I'm friends with know how crucial it is to laugh, play, and truly enjoy life. We incorporate this optimistic and playful mindset into our recreational activities as well as our employment.

Without laughter and fun, all the profits wouldn't have nearly the same sweet taste. In my opinion, a playful attitude is one of the core fundamentals needed for success.

PROFITABLE PLAY

The importance of a playful attitude and childish fun in your daily life is massively overlooked by far too many in the world today. Not only do I believe your daily life should be action-packed with fun, but I firmly believe that your main source of income should be derived from an activity that you thoroughly enjoy doing. Without pure enjoyment from your occupation, it's doubtful that you are truly happy in life.

Now don't get me wrong. I'm not trying to put down anyone's livelihood or business, and I'm aware that sometimes people are stuck working lame jobs.

That's life. Most of us have been there.

However, never again could I imagine myself bitterly punching in or out of a time clock for a job that I didn't enjoy. I just don't see it happening. Hopefully, you won't have to go through this dilemma either.

MR. ABNORMAL

I have to admit, though, that I'm not a normal guy. Somehow, deep within, lies a keen ability for me to find the diamonds in the ruff. Instead of viewing a glass half empty, I see it overflowing.

While many perceive certain situations as problems, I consider them challenges that are worthy of my participation. This change in mindset is crucial for those of you who truly desire success.

Many moons ago I was employed as a dishwasher at the Tabor Hill Café in Portland, Oregon. I truly loved that job. Many people find it odd that I loved being a dishwasher but nothing could be further from the truth. Those days as a greasy dish dog provide some of my fondest memories in life.

First of all, I was madly in love with one of the waitresses at the cafe. She was about six years older than my youthful age of 18, but somehow my silly attitude was able to win her heart.

All the men in their mid 20's and 30's were totally baffled at how a young, rambunctious, tattooed dishwashing punk could get the dream girl they all desired. Every dude in the joint wanted a stab at Erika.

She was drop dead gorgeous.

It was inconceivable that this princess would date a young and silly guy like me. After all, I was just a little kid who rode his skateboard to a peon dishwashing job everyday.

What the other guys in the café failed to realize is that people just want to have fun in life, and that includes Erika. The majority of these men did not enjoy their jobs like I did. Their persona was not attractive. Working in the cooking line, they were too stressed-out.

In my application to the owners, I firmly stated that I wanted no promotions of any kind and wanted to remain the dishwasher for as long as I worked there. I had more then enough qualifications and experience to be a cook, but I preferred to be a dishwasher.

See page 10 for exclusive reader-only FREE offers!

The reason why is very simple. As a dishwasher, the responsibilities were extremely simple. Just keep the darn forks and plates clean and everybody was happy.

There were no hassles, just dishes to wash. It was simple, mindless, and the pay didn't seem bad at the time. People don't have many expectations of the dishwasher other then keeping the plates and utensils clean. That's all I had to do.

In the meantime I was able to spend my time wooing the sexy waitress while the other guys pulled their hair out from all the cooking orders they were constantly getting bombarded with. Meanwhile, I was having fun and getting paid.

WORKING WITH BOOKER T. WASHINGTON

Erika was not the only reason I loved that simple dishwashing job. I had the pleasure of scrubbing plates side by side with an older black man named Booker T. Washington.

This dude was a government conspiracy nut who would continually come to work with some of the greatest reading materials you could ever find. He had this method of highlighting books with five different colored pens, and each color had a specific purpose. Yellow was for quotes, red for interesting facts, and so on.

Spending time with Booker T. made my job absolutely thrilling. Every day I worked with him was riveting, fun, and educational. I love learning, and Booker had some amazing information to study. Sure, tons of the things he said were crazy as hell, but that's what I liked about the guy.

He was willing to question and ask things that 99.9% of the world wouldn't dare touch with a 10 foot pole. Booker helped make my dishwashing job more fun than an amusement park. I'll never forget that guy.

However I have to credit a man named Sylvester for teaching me to actually like dishwashing. When I was 14, I had a job as a dishwasher at a Mexican restaurant named Poncho's. I started as a dishwasher, and worked my way up to prep cook and line cook. At 14 years old, the last place in the world I wanted to be was in the dish room. I desperately desired a promotion so I could get into the kitchen.

When I finally got the promotion into the kitchen it appeared as if I was on top of the world. No longer would I have to slave away over grimy dishes.

What I didn't realize at the time was that the kitchen was 10 times more stressful then the dish room. Luckily, I had the pleasure of knowing Sylvester, a 40 year old Buddhist man who taught me about a few simple things in life.

He started off by giving me a few Herman Hesse books. Demian was the first book followed by Siddhartha. These books were the beginning of life long mental transformation for me. Quickly I realized that happiness had nothing to do with social status, or how much money you made.

Happiness came from within...

Sylvester was the richest guy I had ever met, and he was a minimum wage dishwasher. I will forever cherish what Sylvester taught me as a young lad. I only wish I had spent more time with the guy.

Time is extremely limited in our short lives. Therefore, I highly recommend that you spend as much time as possible doing pleasurable things throughout your life.

Hopefully, while reading this chapter, you will take a few moments of time to analyze your current situation in life and ask yourself,

"Is there anything I could do to make every day a bit more fun?"

Had mentors not challenged me to seek out fun opportunities in life, I might have missed the boat. Fortunately, I've been able to maintain a playful attitude, and have fun during my short stay on this planet. It's imbedded into my core and it's probably the number one reason I've done so well in every industry I've pursued.

RUB OFF ON OTHERS

One of the coolest things about making a conscious decision to inject more fun into your life is the ramifications it can have on other people. Everyone likes to hang out with the fun guy, right? Not too many people are keen on spending the afternoon with a grumpy and negative dude.

When you genuinely emit fun vibes, it rubs off on others. Just a nice little comment could completely enlighten someone's day. A

See page 10 for exclusive reader-only FREE offers!

simple favor might mean the world to another person.

When you are a sincerely fun and loving person, it provides a great joy to know that you can easily brighten someone's day by implementing simple elements of fun and happiness. Sometimes the little things really do matter to other people, and if you really enjoy making people smile, then it's a win-win situation for everybody.

Being a fun and playful person is beneficial in so many different ways; some are obvious, while many other reasons are quite subtle. I believe people need comic relief in life, and any time you can get someone to laugh, you've done a good deed in my eyes.

COMMIT...TODAY

The truth is that almost every single person who is in decent health can commit to some type of fun activity today. There should be nothing holding you back from having an absolute blast if you truly desire happiness.

Sometimes people just need a kick in the rear to get them onto the pathway to fun. Lot's of folks are not in the daily routine of play-fulness and just need a little reminder of how to break loose.

> "Without play - without the child that still lives
> in all of us - we will always be incomplete. And not
> only physically, but creatively, intellectually, and
> spiritually as well." — Dr. George Sheehan

Those beautiful words uttered by Dr. Sheehan remind me of another old teacher of mine. Even though he was 70 years old, Bob sure knew how to play like a young lad. That's what I loved about the old guy.

He was full of life, vibrant, and ready to pounce on the next adventure at any moment. Nothing would stop Bob from achieving whatever he wanted. I was lucky to have absorbed so much from his childlike character.

Please don't discount the advice of being childish. I firmly believe that there is a very pivotal lesson to be learned here. Learn to be childlike in your behavior, and you will continually be blessed with miles of smiles.

Believe it or not, you're likely to make a bunch more money too!

Of course, when I suggest you learn to be childlike, I'm not implying that you should act completely immature and mindless. Business is still business, and you don't want to screw that up.

I'm talking about adopting a mentality that encourages you to seek out fun opportunities around you at all times. The act of playing is beyond just a physical thing. It goes deep into your being.

Once you are able to let go and truly play, it's similar to the results of meditation that many have been struggling to attain for years.

REMOVING LIMITATIONS

When submerged in the act of playing, all problems seem to vanish. Obstacles become part of the game.

No longer are the roadblocks huge annoyances, but they are challenges to overcome. Barriers turn into mazes, and dead ends become unexplored paths to the motherland.

There are no limits to what is possible when you are in full time play mode. But it's not easy to just enter this land of fun and games. It takes an immense amount of practice for some people.

Playing seems so simple, but in reality, getting lost in playfulness is very difficult for some. Simply playing by itself can open a whole new world of enjoyment in your life.

If you are so lucky to find this playful land, it will definitely help to stimulate your creativity. Ideas will bum-rush your cranium when you become truly child like.

When there are no worries about what other people think, and just authentic, driven passion controls you, it's incredibly powerful. The brainstorming potential is endless with a playful person.

There are many reasons why I chose the topics of "Fun" and "Playing" for this "Million Dollar Marketing Secrets" chapter, but there is none more important than your mental health. Personally, I don't find any gratification in having a ton of cash if I'm not entirely happy with my life.

I'd prefer working as a vendor in a professional baseball parking lot for minimum wage before I would accept a full time position at a lame corporation that I didn't truly believe in.

Many businesses and corporations can become emotional roller coasters with gruesome side effects, but it doesn't have to be that way. Most business entrepreneurs have ambitious goals of making it to the big time, yet they often lack knowledge of the core fundamentals of what it takes to create a wildly successful company.

A WILDLY SUCCESSFUL COMPANY

Anyone can become financially successful. That's not too tough. To build a wildly successful company, however, that enriches and benefits all those involved, now that's a sign of true achievement. When you have accomplished this, you have done a great service to yourself and to your fellow man as well. Accomplish this, and you have developed a wildly successful company.

Yesterday, I had an awesome moment while listening to an audio interview with my copywriter friends, Shaune Clarke and Brian Keith Voiles. Brian is a kid at heart who loves to read and create comic books.

Now, that's what I'm talking about! That's the kind of fun we all need in our lives. It might be a comic book, or it could be a video game, or maybe just paddling your boat across the lake. Whatever your idea of fun is, make sure you set aside adequate time in your life for these playful activities.

Brian's enthusiasm was undeniable, magnetic, and full of playfulness. This guy is seriously hyped up on fun stuff. It was extremely comforting to listen to that audio because it was blatantly obvious how much Brian loved his playtime.

He told a story about not wanting to come out of his "Sandbox." I totally understood the analogy he was making. In fact, it might not have been an analogy at all. It would be easy to see Brian actually playing in the sandbox with a bunch of Hot Wheels and sand castle toys. He's not too mature to allow himself to get down-n-dirty in the sandbox and just play.

There is a big difference between trying to be childlike, and actually being 100% consumed with the task at hand. Children don't play and simultaneously think about the mortgage payments, or homework that is due tomorrow. They are completely involved with whatever game they are playing. As adults, it's tough to get into the frame of mind where all worries evaporate. Just acting like a kid doesn't cut it. You have to truly be childlike. You need to be overwhelmed by the joy of playing to forget about real world problems.

If you can achieve this, you have attained the power that so many of us have lost in our lives. We have forgotten how to play.

ME: UNDERACHIEVER OF THE YEAR!

My sophomoric attitude toward business, and my silly nature online, has truly catapulted me to a position that many long for. I doubt I would have won the "Underachiever of the Year" award had I not made silly videos and songs making fun of Frank Kern.

Those acts of child's play are some of the main reasons I've developed online fame. People expect to see me act like an idiot. They want to laugh, and I'm a perfect vehicle for inducing that laughter. Without the humor, idiocy, and silly pranks, it's doubtful I would have nearly the amount of website traffic that currently comes into my sites today. Personally, I wouldn't have it any other way.

I know the last thing you expected to find in this book was some young punk kid telling you to play like you were on the Monkey Bars at the school yard. However, that's exactly what I'm saying to you.

Have some fun with your day. Take your colleagues to the Go-Cart track for lunch today. Maybe you could arrange a company softball game.

You'll be amazed at how productive employees can be when they get to have some outdoor fun together. So please, I'm begging you to explore the avenues of childlike behavior. I promise that your life, business, and relationships with others will be dramatically enriched for the better if you adopt a playful attitude.

Now, get out there and play!

Editor's Note: The chapter submitted for the project by Jason "Profit" Moffatt was nothing like what we were expecting. Yet, when reading it, we found it provocative – and decided to leave it in. Amidst the highly-valuable marketing advice imparted in this book, enjoy this chapter as a moment to reflect on "what's really important."

See page 10 for exclusive reader-only FREE offers!

FREE!
Continue Your Learning And
Business-Building Online:
www.MDMSbonus.com

CHAPTER NINETEEN

The E3 Marketing Mindset

How One Transaction Can Make You Independently Wealthy For Life!

John Nevo

Entrepreneur, Author & Speaker

John Nevo is a family man and entrepreneur who loves to excel in customer service and passionately sell through his true conviction. His experience goes way back to his childhood task and paper routes.

John grew up in a entrepreneurial family that saw riches and then rags. Even though his mom and dad lost everything in the restaurant and night club business, he was determined to succeed and defy the odds.

John saw a need to be different and take extreme pride in simple tasks that would move him ahead of the class. His true customer service translated into sales in the cash register. Something so simple yet impossible to so many people would make the difference. Truly helping his customers before himself would be the magic that makes so much sense, but practiced so little by so many folks.

He practiced these techniques throughout his career in sales ringing up mega sales, profits and many top awards for companies such as Hershey Chocolate, M&M Mars, National Wines, GlaxoSmithKline, Novartis and Cephalon. Incredibly, during this time frame, he finished his college degree from Purdue University, with a Bachelors Degree in Business Management Sciences and took his vending company from a few dollars to over a million dollars! John lives in Indiana and owes his success to his wife Vicki and inspiration with their three children, Brenden, Karmen and Brooklyn.

The Nevo Group

Fort Wayne, IN • 260-432-5260 • www.JohnNevo.com

<u>John Nevo</u>

The E3 Marketing Mindset

How One Transaction Can Make You Independently Wealthy For Life!

Have you ever walked into a store and wanted someone to help you with your problem, but realized you were just a number of many that were trying to get that same attention? If you starve for that type of service that exceeds expectations in everything, then you will want to incorporate the E3 marketing mindset. The E3 marketing mindset will help you profitably market your business while striving for continuous and never ending improvements in product quality, customer service and employee rapport.

I discovered many years ago that people in America genuinely wanted service that cared about their needs and delivered excellence in all fashions. This doesn't mean that mistakes were not allowed. If anything, mistakes were a must to achieve the best service attainable.

I encourage you to take a moment and ponder how your customers view the service you deliver.

- Do you realize how important they are to your business? I can bet that your customers are low hanging fruit for all those other starving vultures.

- Do you have time to take a chance on just average service?

- Do you communicate with your customers frequently and follow up on their needs?

- Do you really take the time to express your gratitude or implement a system that is second to none?

- How do you measure up to your competition?

- Do you know your competition better than you know any of your family members?

If the answer is no and you are getting quite concerned at this point, then it is time to incorporate the E3 mindset.

Your success will be measured by profitable sales growth, extreme customer satisfaction, category leadership, optimal product quality and associate development. This equation will translate into a customer for life.

Earl Nightingale tells a story about a farmer who sold his farm to find wealth and ended up with nothing. However, the gentlemen that bought his property was quite pleased with his purchase. One fine day the man discovered one of the most prized jewels in this world, right on his own property. He discovered the world's largest diamond ever found! The moral to this story is that the diamonds are beneath your feet.

My reference to the farmer is to enhance your creative ability, to dig deeper and discover how important it is to incorporate the E3 marketing mindset. Why, you ask? It is quite simple and I will explain.

Over the last 20 years since the inception of the personal computers and the infamous World Wide Web, people have literally relied on email, the internet and websites to communicate. We have witnessed before our eyes that personal communication and service has disappeared as if David Copperfield snapped his fingers and made it all vanish. It is pretty scary, once you think about it.

We have watched the crashing of American companies and our jobs leave us as if we have given up! It saddens me that we accept mediocre service and faulty products for high prices, but yet we just sit there and do nothing. If this is motivating you and you want to take back America and the leading country in this world, then it is time to incorporate the E3 marketing mindset.

The competitive advantage is right at your fingertips and it's slipping away fast. Do you want to set yourself apart and excel to the head of the class? If so, you must read on! In approximately 2 years, over 70 million Americans will turn 62! Will you be ready? The early baby boomers have literally seen it all and heard it all. They believe in hard work and have worked hard to get the fortunes they incorporate. They will search out for the best of the best and then deter-

See page 10 for exclusive reader-only FREE offers!

mine where they will spend their money. I will give you a quick example! My father-in-law, or "dad" for short, recently made a purchase that blew me away. He bought an in-ground sprinkler system that cost him over $5,000.00 to water his lawn, plants and flowers. I was stunned in silence and my thoughts pondered. I proceeded to ask my dad what possessed him to make such a purchase. This was not the same man I thought I knew. The man I knew would have dragged the hose around the yard until the job was done. "Son", he said, "I have worked all my life and your mother and I are retired and both still recovering from back surgery. They installed everything and they come out at the end of the season to blow the lines out. In the spring, they come back out and turn them on, plus repair any winter damaged sprinkler heads." "For free," I shouted! "No silly," he said! "I will pay them for that service." I smiled and nodded with excitement. My guess was right.

That was the answer I was looking for and validated my system that I have practiced for years. It had truly come full circle. The time is now to incorporate the E3 marketing mindset. The necessary steps and goals must be implemented in your marketing playbook to exceed excellence in everything.

1. Leadership

2. Vision

3. Customer Target Market

4. Analysis Management

5. Customer Service

6. Infrastructure

7. Results

Leadership is a deciding factor that determines the organization's responsibility to itself and to all its customers in a fashion that enrobes itself with integrity, trust and wellbeing. This will set the stage for continuous and never ending improvement. It will be important to develop a code of ethics that assures the companies direction that provides an excellent shopping experience for all its customers. Quality leaders lead by example and strive for excellence everyday. The leader will possess character that has established rapport and consistency. He or she will focus on helping others to get what they want and deliver a feel good attitude. They will also push forward with their 100% commitment for success. Strong leaders will possess courage, competency and positive wisdom. Dedicated leadership will focus on the power of listening that translates into powerful relationships which follow to achieve the common goal.

Vision is the marketing backbone that translates a dream into reality. It provides a road map that allows yourself and your associates to work together and achieve excellence in everything. It will possess the values necessary to fulfill those dreams. It will provide confidence and establish goal setting that leads to the success of all the marketing concepts of the E3 marketing mindset.

Remember the vision that Walt Disney had to develop Walt Disney World. It all began with a mouse and a man who had a vision to turn a dream into reality by bringing family members together to enjoy and have fun.

The customer target market provides a direction to the population where your company and products will exist. It will consist of data that helps you identify your customer's wants and needs. It is often defined by the age, gender and social economic grouping. This will be done through proper farming and marketing analysis. It will be important to understand your customer's buying habits too. This will allow you to develop products that match the market segment you wish to focus. It will be broken down into three steps; market segmentation, customer focus and brand positioning or a particular niche. Strategies that you develop will be based on your competition, consumer demand, and the profitability of your product.

Your analysis management, or SWOT analysis, is a powerful technique for understanding your strengths and weaknesses, and for looking at the opportunities and threats you face. This concept is very powerful because it can help you uncover opportunities that you are well placed to take advantage of and by understanding the weaknesses of your business, you can manage and eliminate the threats that catch you off guard. Also, by looking at yourself and your competitors using the SWOT infrastructure, this will allow you to separate yourself from your competitors so that you can compete successfully in your market.

See page 10 for exclusive reader-only FREE offers!

STRENGTHS: TAKE A MOMENT
TO LIST YOUR STRENGTHS

For example:

- What advantages does your company or product have?

- What do you do better than everyone else?

- What are your resources?

- What do your mentors or people in your market see as your strengths?

In looking at your strengths, it is important to know your competitors fully, because an appeared strength may just be a necessity to operate your business.

WEAKNESSES: TAKE A MOMENT
TO LIST YOUR WEAKNESSES

For example:

- What areas can you improve?

- What areas or objections should you avoid?

- What do your mentors or people in your market see as your weaknesses?

In looking at your weaknesses, ask yourself, are they your perceived weaknesses or your customer's views? Can a weakness be an opportunity to improve the market segmentation you are currently in? State the facts and be realistic to yourself. Focus on your strengths that differentiate yourself from your competitors.

OPPORTUNITIES: TAKE A MOMENT
TO LIST YOUR OPPORTUNITIES

For example:

- Do you have existing knowledge?

- Is technology on your side?

- Has a recent competitor failed to deliver the process you can do better?

- Is there a new life event that supports growth and change in the market?

- Are you first to market?

Based on the opportunities that exists in your life today, it is important to capitalize now and take advantage of the success and strike when the coal is hot.

THREATS: TAKE A MOMENT TO LIST YOUR THREATS

For example:

- What road blocks do you face?

- What is your competition doing?

- Do you have the resources to compete?

- Could any of your weaknesses threaten your business?

There are perceived threats and real threats. List them in order of importance and try to eliminate them in chronological order. This will allow you to focus on what moves your business forward. Remember, if what you are doing today is not moving your business forward, don't do it.

Customer service is your ultimate weapon when competing head on with your competition. It is important to realize that customer relations mirror employee relations. They invest heavily in their people and provide believable career paths. It translates into heroes on the front lines and reaps the rewards of low turnover and high performance. Customer service will be the rise or fall of your business. A customer service program is easy to implement and hard to maintain.

See page 10 for exclusive reader-only FREE offers!

For example:

- A mission statement that is customer focused
- Creating a VIP member status or best customer program
- A marketing program that communicates with you customer frequently
- A recognition program for employees and customers
- Continuous and never ending improvement through training
- Reliable products and or service
- Responsiveness to the customer or situation
- Allow the customer to voice their opinion and take notes
- Thank your customer continuously and give them something free

It is important to instill the vision from the top to the bottom of your company through communication and employee gratification.

Infrastructure is the road map or elements that provide the framework to support your business. Imagine the process of building a house and transcend that application into your business. The land or platform must be clear and concise, free of any fragments or debris that would allow for a smooth foundation. The foundation is secured with proper footers and slabs to ensure stability in the structure. Then the walls are built to enclose the house as are the guidelines to your business. The roof is constructed to seal the home and foundation of your business. The inside of your house is broken into many rooms as the departments of your business. Each department, as your house, will consist of fine detail that decorates and describes your platform or finish to your house or business.

The results of your company are based on your customer's response and profitable sales. If you have taken the time to thoroughly follow my marketing plan, then you may be successful in your business. The results of your business can be properly tuned as your business progresses. This may involve product implementation, price and ad copy that sells the product. A small business can implement improvement in quality, whether in service, a product, or values. Be consistent, dependable and a powerful resource to all walks of life.

I'd like to reference one final story. When my wife was a former travel agent we had the unforgettable experience of touring behind the scenes of the Ritz Carlton in Cancun, Mexico. During this time, they were eligible for the Malcolm Baldrige Award.

Congress established this award in 1987 to honor U.S. organizations for their achievements and to raise awareness about the importance of quality and performance excellence as a competitive edge. It's named after Malcolm Baldrige who was Secretary of Commerce from 1981 until his death in a rodeo accident in 1987. Baldrige was a proponent of quality management as a key to America's prosperity and long-term strength.

Each year, the U.S. President gives three awards in the categories of manufacturing, service, small business, education, and health care to recipients who have been judged as outstanding.

The Baldrige Award recognizes a standard of excellence that helps American organizations achieve world-class quality. It's designed to help organizations enhance their competitiveness by focusing on the deliverance of ever improving value to customers and by improving overall organizational performance. These criteria have played a major role in achieving the goals established by Congress and are now widely accepted the world over as the standard for performance excellence.

In October 2004, President Bush signed legislation authorizing the U.S. Commerce Department's National Institute of Standards and Technology (NIST) to expand the program to include non-profit and government organizations.

Baldrige Award winners take their role as quality advocates very seriously. Recipients have given tens of thousands of presentations reaching thousands of organizations. Their efforts to educate and inform companies and organizations about the benefits of using the Baldrige Award framework and criteria have far exceeded expectations.

The purpose in explaining the Baldrige Award is to understand the experience my wife and I encountered at this amazing resort. It has forever impacted me in my beliefs and expectations of the businesses or customers I do business with today.

You can see how important it is to have an E3 marketing mindset. That is, exceeding expectations in everything! I wish you good fortune and good luck as you strive for excellence in everything you do.

See page 10 for exclusive reader-only FREE offers!

FREE!

**Continue Your Learning And
Business-Building Online:
www.MDMSbonus.com**

CHAPTER TWENTY

The Yellow Pages Dilemma

How to face your competition head-on, and attract a steady stream of new business

Alan Saltz

Renowned Yellow Pages Expert

How do you capitalize on perfectly targeted, ready-to-buy prospects when you're surrounded by your fiercest competition? Business owners all over the world have turned to Wharton graduate, Yellow Pages advertising strategist and author Alan Saltz, for the answer.

"In the Yellow Pages you're rarely, if ever, the only provider of a particular product or service" says Saltz, author of *Yellow Pages Profit*. "But, with the right ad content, you can credibly differentiate your company, and stand out as the obvious choice."

Alan Saltz uncovers:

- The difference between the Yellow Pages and other advertising medium
- The one thing a Yellow Pages ad must do to be effective
- The cardinal sin of Yellow Pages advertising and how to avoid it
- The 3 vital components for increasing response
- How to jump off the page and engage your prospect
- How to remove skepticism and develop trust
- How to motivate a prospect to take immediate action

Guaranteed Marketing, Inc.
New York, NY • 1-877-243-9612 • www.YellowPagesProfit.com

Alan Saltz

The Yellow Pages Dilemma
How to face your competition head-on, and attract a steady stream of new business

Yellow Pages Advertising: three words that instill frustration and doubt in the minds of business owners all over the world. And then there's me - who has been absolutely, positively enamored by the medium. Why? Let me put it this way...

No one turns on the radio or TV and hollers, "Ooh, let's get to them commercials already!" No one hops into their car to read the billboard ads plastered above the highway. And no one opens their mail in eager anticipation of the offers that are waiting for them.

And yet - every day like clockwork - thousands of people across the globe flock to the Yellow Pages with the sole purpose of finding an ad (and a company) that catches their attention. That's a major difference.

In fact, the Yellow Pages is a contender for the most targeted advertising medium on the planet. Just about everyone who takes the time to open up that big yellow book is an attentive and qualified prospect, *who is ready to make a buying decision!* To put your business in front of eyes like these is very powerful indeed.

So why all the uncertainty? For one, the expense and full year commitment is intimidating. Secondly, it's highly competitive. After all, every time a prospect turns to your category, they're there to choose between you and everybody else.

The obvious solution - and the purpose of this chapter - is to identify proven and ethical ways to out-smart, out-class, and out-perform the competition... so that when a qualified prospect turns to your category, your ad will deliver the results you're looking for.

THE "PURPOSE" OF YOUR YELLOW PAGES AD

The goal of your ad is to attract a steady flow of new customers to your business. Of course, the Yellow Pages adds the element of competition, pitting you against other companies who provide the same products and services you do.

You're an option. They are too.

In other words, it's not enough to simply talk about the products and services you provide if you're hoping to get "more than your fair share" of calls. You actually have to stand out as a **different** - and **better** - option than the competition!

To repeat, you're a plumber. They're plumbers too. But somehow, you need to differentiate your company in a positive way. So, when a prospect has viewed ten ads including your own, they're saying to themselves, **"This company is different... I prefer to do business with them."**

The purpose of your ad is to create this preference. Seems obvious enough, but as you're about to uncover, most ads are "missing the boat" entirely.

I want you to open up the Yellow Pages and turn to any category that comes to mind. (Really, go grab it!) Now, try to spot a **real difference** in the ads you see. In fact, jot down all of the important details that you see in one ad that you don't see in any other.

What you'll likely find is that aside from the items that literally define a company - the company name, logo and contact information for example - the ads say essentially the same thing.

You'll find a number of overused slogan-like statements that lack impact and credibility - like "the carpet specialists," "prompt friendly service," and "put our experience to work for you," and a long "laundry-list" of the products and services offered - which needless to say, are common to every advertiser in the category.

What you *rarely* find, is a company that **credibly differentiates themselves** as a different and better option than the competition. The adoption of this "me-too" mentality is the cardinal sin of Yellow Pages advertising! You cannot increase call quality and frequency if you look and sound like everybody else.

See page 10 for exclusive reader-only FREE offers!

BECOME YOUR CUSTOMER

Take a moment to put yourself in the mind of someone turning to your Yellow Pages category. Remember, as honest and skilled as you are, your prospect doesn't know you, and just because you say you're "The Most Trusted Name In…" doesn't make it so.

As consumers, we've all been burned. We've been promised things that have not been delivered. There have been catches, fine print, and hidden fees. And so, it's no surprise that your prospects are skeptical when they turn to your subject heading. That's where good ad content comes in.

Effective ad content will remove this skepticism and convince your prospects that you are someone they want to do business with. Since I've already discussed what's not believable and what doesn't work, let's get to what does.

VITAL AD COMPONENT #1: A STRONG HEADLINE

Nothing does more to make your company
stand out than a strong headline.

Believe it or not, this opportunity is wasted by a vast majority of advertisers, who instead, do one of two things: 1) Use their company name and logo 2) Choose a vague slogan-like statement. Neither of these choices have an impact on a buying decision.

Here are a few real life examples of ineffective, overused headlines pulled directly from my local Yellow Pages:

- "Excellence You Can Trust"

- "Digital Hearing Aid Experts"

- "Duct Cleaning Specialists"

Do these headlines really say anything believable? Since the two roles of a headline are to grab attention, and to compel a prospect to read more, you'll see how they fail on both accounts.

Now consider these headlines:

For a Personal Injury Attorney:

For a plumber:

For a mover:

You should notice how these headlines draw a prospect into the rest of the ad. They make someone care what you have to say!

If you were in a car accident, loaded with questions and concerns as you search for an attorney, wouldn't you find that first headline impossible to ignore? You'd want to know what **one question** is so important. That headline gives the attorney an opportunity to educate his prospect, and to put some of his fears to rest. Compare that to the overused headline, "Put Our Experience on Your Side" followed by a list of injury cases handled. There's just no question which will create more preference.

The second ad uses a strong trust-building policy that's more believable than any slogan.

The third headline engages the reader with a question, and even

See page 10 for exclusive reader-only FREE offers!

tells a story. You'll notice again, how it draws a prospect into the ad to find out what makes this company different and better. The prospect's attention has been grabbed, and they are primed and perceptive to all of the reasons this mover will be a choice they feel good about.

To reiterate, your headline must do two things:

- Grab attention and make your ad pop off the page (make it big and bold)

- Compel the prospect to read the rest of the ad

VITAL AD COMPONENT #2: BENEFIT-LADEN BODY COPY

The goal of your body copy is to build a prospect's perception of your company.

It needs to provide a strong and believable answer to the question, "Why should I do business with you instead of with your competition?"

As you now know, a list of products and services merely proves that you are an option, not the best option. That's not to say it shouldn't be in your body copy, but it shouldn't be the focus. Rather, you should focus on the benefits of doing business with you...

- The policies you hold yourself to that prove you're fair and honest.

- Those things you offer that your competitors do not.

- Solutions to the concerns and fears you know your clients have.

Policies make for great Yellow Pages content for the simple reason that they're believable. They also show that you have your customers' best interests in mind. The vague statement "We're Prompt" is not a policy. It lacks credibility and it's quickly forgotten. But this isn't: "On-time guaranteed, or we'll deduct 10% off our fee."

Someone I know actually advertised that he gives away 2 free movie tickets every time he arrived outside of his one hour appointment window. That's a brilliant idea! That policy assures his customers that he understands how valuable their time is. It says something about him and how he does business.

Here are a few more examples of strong policies:

- Quotes in writing before work begins. No hidden fees! No surprises!
- All work owner supervised and 100% satisfaction & results guaranteed.
- Ask about our no-pressure computer-generated closet design consultation.
- Our employees undergo thorough background testing and ongoing training.

Think about how this kind of ad content elevates your perception of a company and paints a "positive mental picture." That's a vital component to generating a phone call.

Naturally, awards, affiliations, and achievements can also create preference in the mind of your prospect. What have you done that your competitors have not? What newspapers or magazines have you been featured in? What trust-building affiliations do you have?

- "Voted the #1 Insurance Agency by the Lexington Bugle."

- Dr. Bay is a nationally recognized speaker on the topic of advanced neck care.

- An upstanding member of the Better Business Bureau for 16 years.

A third great example of benefit-laden body content - is anything you offer that's more advanced or powerful than what your competition is offering. If your carpet, powerwash, insulation, or roofing product or technology is more effective than a competing product, say it! If you're a doctor using a new and better technology, talk about it!

- Our unique "FlexLight" windows reduce cooling bills by up to 34%.

- One of only a few back specialists in Dallas using new pain-free laser technology.

A small box explaining how your product/service is superior to others on the market can be very effective addition to your ad.

It's a good idea to organize the rest of your benefits into a bulleted list so they work together to create a positive mental picture.

See page 10 for exclusive reader-only FREE offers!

Like this...

5 Reasons Dallas Homeowners Insist on XYZ Carpets

- Fixed Price Quotes - *in writing* - before work begins
- Our truckmount technology dries faster and *repels stains*
- *Background-checked*, well groomed (& friendly) technicians
- Our iron-clad $20 on-time guarantee... and *results guarantee*
- Rug pickup & delivery is a *free* and "no-tips accepted" service

Another great idea is to use the technique I employed in the mover ad in the previous category, and outline your benefits in what I refer to as a "post-headline" paragraph. It's more conversational... it "speaks" to the prospect... and it gives them a real insight into the person (or persons) behind the company. Very few ads do this and it can be a very powerful technique.

To review, the purpose of your body content is to provide people with real reasons to prefer you over your competition. Be specific. Be believable. Be personal. The more you set yourself apart from your competition in a positive way, the more you increase phone call frequency and quality.

VITAL AD COMPONENT #3: A STRONG CALL TO ACTION

The call to action is a vital ad component that's rarely used. This is especially surprising given the level of competition advertisers face in the Yellow Pages. So, the question begs to be asked, "What is it worth to you to get someone to choose you instead of a competitor? What are you prepared to offer them?"

The call to action is literally an order to pick up the phone for a specific reason; the better the reason, the greater the impetus to follow your instructions.

By creating an effective call to action, you can literally put words into your prospects mouth as they pick up the phone. You plant a seed. You give them something specific to inquire about when they hear your voice on the other end of the line. Simply stated, tell them to:

- "Call now for..."
- "Call now and ask about..."
- "Mention this ad when you call to receive..."

You can prompt someone to call for more information about something you've discussed in your ad (like a free report, "The 5 Things the Insurance Companies Don't Want You to Know!" or "The Complete Guide to Surgery-Free Laser Therapy") or there's always a freebie, or special offer that can be extended:

- Call now and receive a free bucket of golf balls with 18 holes!

- Call now to receive $50 OFF your bathroom remodel!

- Mention this ad for a FREE universal remote with TV repair!

The greater the perceived value of your offer, the more effective it will be. So as an aside to business owners who enjoy a great deal of repeat business or referrals - you should be willing to give a lot more to get a new customer in the door, as your profit potential extends far beyond the purpose of their current call.

One last thing. The industry standard "free estimate" or "free consultation" is not a strong call to action because everyone is offering it. It's perceived as the norm. Come up with something more compelling to use in conjunction with that, and you'll increase the perceived value of picking up the phone to call your company.

CONCLUSION

There's been a common theme running through the sections of this chapter that can be summarized by two words. Differentiate yourself. Being an option will never equate to better-than-average results, especially when you consider that ad size plays a role in response.

So don't blend in. Stand out. Make sure your ad content makes you a more credible, more approachable, more value-filled solution than the competition. Be certain that you've provided real and specific reasons to prefer your company over all of the others.

When you do, you've given your prospects a standard of comparison that's far more beneficial to you than price comparison. And that... is a wonderful thing.

See page 10 for exclusive reader-only FREE offers!

FREE!
**Continue Your Learning And
Business-Building Online:
www.MDMSbonus.com**

CHAPTER TWENTY-ONE

Your Company Name Here!

How to Turn Freebies Into Profitable Promotions

Melanie Sibbitt

President and Head Crazy Lady

Back in the last century, 1988 to be exact, Melanie Sibbitt co-founded Two Crazy Ladies Inc. with just one product, a Doodle Mug™. After the first year, her partner left but she carried on, growing Two Crazy Ladies Inc. into a business offering over one million products.

She coaches clients on optimum ways to invest in promotional items they give away for free as a strategy for making more money in their business.

"Yes, you can make more money by strategically giving stuff away for free," says Sibbitt. "However, too many clients throw money away, handing out the wrong items to the wrong people."

"I'm very proud that our team of highly qualified, creative and fun people consistently help clients develop the most effective programs," Sibbitt adds.

Melanie Sibbitt:
- Served on the Board for the Promotional Products Association of Canada
- Served on the Board for The Women Entrepreneurs of Canada
- Was nominated for the Canadian Women Entrepreneur of the Year Awards
- Is active in philanthropy...Worked to send Easter Seals Kids to camp and helped raise money in the fight against Breast Cancer through the Golf for The Cure program

Two Crazy Ladies Inc.
Toronto, ON, CA • 1-800-735-2654 • www.twocrazyladies.com

Melanie Sibbitt

Your Company Name Here!
How to Turn Freebies Into Profitable Promotions

Ever used "freebies" to promote your business?

I proudly produce freebies... promotional products used as give-aways to:

- Incite trial

- Incentivize participation

- Deepen bonds with existing clients

- Build loyalty

Sometimes promotional items cost hundreds of dollars, often times pennies, but they should never be cheap. The strategy of promotions is to give an appropriate gift to a thirsty target audience.

If you have doubts about including promotions in your marketing strategy, consider this recent survey of travelers at Dallas/Fort Worth airport:

- 71% of travelers received a promo product in the last year

- 76% of these could remember who gave them the promo

- 34% actually had the item on them.

Isn't this the kind of relationship you'd love to build with your customers and prospects?

MAY I PAY YOU $100?

If you show me an older example of a promotional item in America I'll send you $100...

The First American Promotional Items

George Washington, Founding Father of the United States and-Founding Father of the promotional products industry? Strange, but true! The oldest known items manufactured in North America for promotional purposes are the wide array of brass and copper buttons made to commemorate Washington's inaugural.

Washington was one savvy marketer, who sensed that the historic occasion should be celebrated with flair. He ordered a custom-made set of gilt buttons engraved with eagles, which he wore on that momentous day. The emblematic bird was already an icon in 1789.

A large selection of other buttons were produced (which were worn by inserting the shanks into buttonholes). Though expensive, they were snapped up by well-heeled Colonials eager to honor their first president. What's even more amazing, is how modern in concept most of those buttons are. Many sport the initials GW in what amounts to a logo, and are surrounded by the slogan: Long Live the President.

GW-do you suppose anyone called him that?-instinctively knew how to brand himself, something today's strategic business owners admire.

Further leveraging promotional items, during Washington's run for a second term he created the first campaign buttons, engraved with his initials, helping friends and followers show their support and share their favor.

See page 10 for exclusive reader-only FREE offers!

Washington saw that wearable promotions made his message reach broader audiences and helped his meetings feel larger and more unified.

After Washington, the promotional products industry grew slowly. By the end of the 19th Century you could see burlap school bags,   calendars, hats for horses, bags for marbles, buggy whips, flyswatters and buttonhooks. (Those fancy buttons were tricky to attach.)

Fast forward to the 21st century, and it's difficult to imagine any home or office without some promotional items on display. (Have you read your kids' T-shirts lately?) But today's brandable products have far surpassed your father's Snap-On Tools calendar. Think holographic mousepads or leather encased portable computer memory sticks-makes me wish my brain had a USB port! And for James Bond wannabes, how about an MP3 pen? This cool gizmo is a fully functional MP3 player and voice recorder with a built-in speaker that plays 512 megs of tunes (and a message from you) to keep you right in the palm of your client.

To see photos of these cool products, please visit
www.twocrazyladies.com

HAVE YOU SEEN OUR WALLABY?

When the Aussie wine [yellow tail] flew into Canada, they started with a corkscrew promotion for restaurant and bar owners before going mass. This is common strategy: *start with gifts to the industry and category mavens and then go for a more mass promotion for consumers.*

[yellow tail] commissioned a custom-made bottle stopper used as a value-added gift with purchase. Since their logo is a colorful wallaby (your basic cute little kangaroo) I had one sculpted for the top of the stopper. This was a huge success, and wine merchants reported they couldn't keep the bottles on their shelves.

THEY CAN SEE CLEARLY NOW

Palm Canada wanted to instill a long-lasting reminder of Treo, a handheld PDA they were launching to their dealer network. We imprinted the Palm logo on a durable microfiber cleaning cloth, which is used on eyeglasses, computer screens and other high-tech gadgets. The 8,000 customer service reps who received the cleaning cloth, appreciated getting something they could use on their job.

IF YOU'RE NOT GIVING STUFF AWAY, YOU'RE HOLDING YOUR COMPANY BACK

Nothing matches the WOW factor of promoting your company with strategically branded gifts, hey, everybody likes a nice present-nice being the key word. Handing out junk will only net you a junky reputation. But rewarding loyal clients or effective employees with quality items wins you big points. Here's a quick list of when this form of marketing is so effective...

When are FREEBIES strategic?

Promotions are strategic when they increase your overall profitability...

- Reinforce your message...Match the item to your message and you reinforce your major sales point

- To stay top-of-mind...tools or something fun to share are often kept for years, plus they're just plain fun to give and you gain wonderful goodwill

- Over Christmas glasses boxed with a bottle magically becomes a gift... these strategically designed promos create an instant "gift" and motivate topical sales

- When you want to maximize energy...Perfect way to promote a launch or celebrate an anniversary, because promotional items create an excuse to talk about what's topical, reinforce themes and give specific support points and provide contact information

- Employee bonding...positive recognition and public praise is prized more than financial rewards by most employees so give them an award they're proud to display

See page 10 for exclusive reader-only FREE offers!

MATCHING THE ITEM TO THE MESSAGE

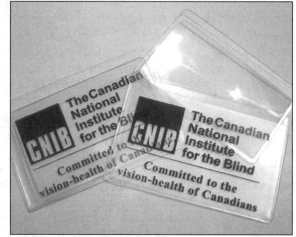

When the Canadian National Institute for the Blind needed an item they could send out inside a fundraising, I suggested a pocket magnifier. Their main concern was that the weight of the item didn't increase the cost of the mailing, so this was ideal. The size of a credit card, it came in a vinyl sleeve sporting the organization logo. The clear plastic magnifier was a perfect match for their message about helping your vision and helping them magnify their ability to help others.

You see how the promotional item reinforces their main message? Match the item to your message. This promotion was so successful, they're doing it again this year.

TOP-OF-MIND CAN BE SUSTAINED THROUGH THEIR HANDS-ON EXPERIENCE

A favorite product to brand is a squeezable, rubber stress toy-from light bulbs to lightning bolts, from dolphins to donuts. A woman who received a colorful, squeezable brain at a conference, expressed her thanks: "I use it many times a day to combat arthritis, and seeing your URL flexing in my hand often inspires me to revisit your website." There's a customer for life!

CELEBRATIONS SHOULD BE FUN — MAXIMIZE THE ENERGY

Are you looking for a fun way to launch a new company or product, or celebrate an anniversary? Imagine taking eight of your best clients to a private box at your local baseball park:

1. Get things rolling with an invitation written on a baseball

2. Continue to build anticipation for the event by sending them baseball caps and little baseball gloves

3. During the game you'll enjoy all the traditional food: popcorn, beer and hotdogs

4. Finally top-off the night with a thank you gift of a premium stadium blanket, embroidered with your company logo

Okay, I did this for myself. Nine years later, people still tell me they're using the blanket, and best of all, every customer who attended that party is still a client today. Gee, it's not too soon to start thinking about my 20th anniversary!

You see how small promotional items can really make a larger promotional item much more effective. Each promotional give-away should be an expression of you caring for your client or prospect.

INCENTIVES CAN BE EARNED WITH POINTS... SELLING MORE OF YOUR PRODUCT

Use a point system to reward the salespeople or dealers based on their performance.

Olymel, a pork and poultry supplier to Dairy Queen, Wendy's and others, ran a sales incentive program for dealers who had a 10% sales increase from the previous year. Each year sales went up. What drove the promotion is that we picked all brand-name products, so the winners knew they weren't getting cut-rate merchandise. One year, when Olymel was promoting "Love Me Tenders™" chicken strips, the logo for the campaign was a chicken dressed up like Elvis. So a favorite prize I designed was a wool and leather jacket with a huge appliqué of the Elvis chicken.

See page 10 for exclusive reader-only FREE offers!

NEED AN EXCUSE TO VISIT DISTRIBUTORS OR MEET NEW PROSPECTS?

Another way Olymel builds relationships is by dropping off delightful chicken and pig collectibles: piggy banks, pig cookie jars, chicken and pig pens, chicken-shaped stress balls and beanie babies of pigs and chickens.

The right item mailed to targeted prospects can result in great sales, or in this case, donations to the Multiple Sclerosis Society. For over 10 years in a row, MS has conducted a direct mail campaign, sending out a mini screwdriver with a letter explaining how MS affects people, and that they were raising money for research. The card attached to the screwdriver talked about finding the right tool to cure MS. Even such a small item can be imprinted with the MS logo. It was one of their most successful fundraiser campaigns ever.

BE STRATEGIC!
TOP TIPS FOR A SUCCESSFUL
PROMOTIONAL CAMPAIGN

1. Plan how you will distribute your cool promo items; just winging a flying disc to anyone who passes by at a trade show is not your best bet. Your promo expert can offer lots of different strategies...for free reports on how to use promo products effectively, please go here: www.twocrazyladies.com/freeReports

2. Choose promotional items you'd be proud to use or display yourself...it is better to have 100 mugs you are proud of than 5,000 crappy cups that people will throw away-remember, this is going to have your name on it; it represents your company to your clients and you want them to cherish your gift

3. Remember to marry your promo item to your brand or your campaign message. Just sending someone a hat for no apparent reason won't create a lasting impression. Inviting clients to a beach party with a colorful visor or beach ball will.

4. Professional distributors like Two Crazy Ladies Inc. can save you time and money, oversee quality control and make sure you get your lanyards or your letter openers on time. We also add a much needed dose of strategic creativity to your decision making process. We help you look great and feel smart.

Is there a moral to these ideas? Yes. **When you give a little something, you get a lot back.**

DO YOU WANT THE GOOD NEWS, THE BAD NEWS OR THE GREAT NEWS?

Let's start with the good news: There are over a million different promotional items available to choose from, so there's sure to be something just right for your business.

The bad news: There are over a million to choose from!

Okay, so what's the great news? That there are also lots of experts out there to advise you on the right kind of product to meet your marketing goals. When you work with a promo professional, we help you sort them all out, and if we can't find what you want, we'll have it made.

I'm honored to work with so many dynamic partners who are willing to try something different when we suggest you put *Your Company Name Here.*

Some of the statistical facts are reproduced from PPAI.

See page 10 for exclusive reader-only FREE offers!

FREE!

Continue Your Learning And
Business-Building Online:
www.MDMSbonus.com

CHAPTER TWENTY-TWO

Micro Budget Marketing for Maximum Profits!

Proven Tricks That Create a Flood of New Sales Without Spending Hardly a Bean on Marketing!

Alan Forrest Smith

Self Confessed Non Conformist Marketer.
Copywriter, Author, Consultant,
Teacher, Lecturer and More!

A hairdresser for nearly 20 years to acclaimed maverick marketing consultant, huge demand copywriter in less time than it takes to pay of your average car loan! Alan who is also featured on SKY TV has an impressive track record to say the least, for an ex-hairdresser.

- $1.2 million from one simple sales letter series for a car co
- $350,000 in less than 12 hours from a simple fax mailer
- 47% response rate from one single sales letter
- $500,000 from new start up with zero marketing budget!
- 189% increase for a seminar co. in less than 24 hours.
- 1,400% increase after making simple webpage changes
- 400 plus ticket sales from a failed webpage
- $88,000 in sales after tweaking 6 words in a short email
- $84,000 in sales from one 300 word email
- $60,000 slashed from advertising budget in 20 minutes

Need I say more?

Alan is now in huge demand as a consultant, copywriter, marketing man and world traveled public speaker. Alan now hosts his own acclaimed training camps (with over 200 raving testimonials) for copywriting and marketing.

Everything you must know about Alan's marketing co. can be found at www.OrangeBeetle.com where you can subscribe to Alan's own premium newsletter at no charge.

Non Conformist Marketing

Manchester, England • Fax: +441 925 764 422 • www.OrangeBeetle.com

Alan Forrest Smith

Micro Budget Marketing for Maximum Profits!

Proven Tricks That Create a Flood of New Sales Without Spending Hardly a Bean on Marketing!

There's always a time when businesses just don't have cash in the bank for marketing. What do you do?

Clients come to me and say "Look, this is what we have. This is our business model but we're not growing. We don't have the percent of profits of all the things we need fast enough."

To survive in business in 2007 we need to grow super fast or we die. One of the biggest mistakes I find with most businesses is that they waste money on nothing un-measurable marketing.

I'm going to talk about what I've seen and what I've implemented for some of my clients. I'm going to give you some fast track tips that will help you to get off the ground and rolling, really, really fast.

HARD DRIVING YOUR EXISTING CLIENT BASE TO SNOWBALL SALES!

Business owners often overlook the most obvious and profitable sources for new sales. When they need to attract new clients, they think "advertise" first. They think, "We could take out a £5,000 quarter-page advert in the local newspaper and hope that's going to bring us in one or two clients."

I repeatedly come across people who continually search for new clients rather than use their existing client base. Yet new business can easily be grown at warp speed.

Let's look at what clients we have and how we can actually use clients to grow the business super fast. These are just usual things, for example, how much does the average customer spend through the business a year? How can we increase their average spend?

Example:

Let me give you one quick example of what I did with a car sales place. These guys were selling sports cars like they were going out of fashion. Yet they would never, ever dare to offer anything extra. If you're in the mindset of buying something like a sports car, you're not just buying a sports car. You're buying something that just looks mega cool. If you're paying £70,000 for a vehicle, you don't care about the price. You want the biggest wheels, the biggest exhaust system, the noisiest engine. And if it means actually paying an extra few dollars a month, you couldn't care less.

They would lower all these big wheels and the usual stuff that you do when you get parts. So I said to these guys, "How often do you sell these?" They said, "We never sell anything. They're paying a lot for the car so why would they want to spend money on wheels, lowering, and body kits?"

I said, "That's exactly what these people want to buy and all you have to say to them is, "While you're spending £70,000 on this Porsche why don't you have a look at these because they're going to make the car look unbelievable." They think "Hang on, I could have these wheels for an extra £10 a month." For the price of a Starbucks, you can look even better on the road.

It's not about money.

Let's look at the bigger effect. These guys are selling 50 sports cars a week, and they increased their average spend by all these different sets of wheels, sets of interiors, sets of lowering, and springs. Isn't that going to increase their business overnight? All they have to do is have one staff meeting and say "Listen guys, this is what we're going to do. Every time you sell a set of these wheels for £1,500 I'm going to give you £100." It's the old McDonald's thing, "Would you like fries with these?" It's exactly the same.

The bottom line is that there's nothing new here. It's all about leveraging from an existing database of buyers. Even if most businesses never pulled in another new client, they could create a moun-

See page 10 for exclusive reader-only FREE offers!

tainous change in profits overnight by simply getting to grips with their existing database.

Upsell Everything...

When I used to have hairdressing salons we used to always upsell on everything. For example, what we used to do was say to the client, "Your hair's going to look great cut like this, but it's going to look drop dead gorgeous with this color on it, and rather than you come in again next week and pay £70, I'll do it right now for £40. The take up on that in our salon was virtually 100% percent. I've since trained hundreds of salons all over the world to do exactly the same and the reports that come flooding back are just unbelievable. It's so easy all this stuff. It's not rocket science at all.

CULTIVATE CUSTOMER TRUST AND RELATIONSHIPS USING SIMPLE DATABASE BUILDING

So many businesses deal with clients on a robotic level, and don't understand that you have to have a relationship with them. When you go to buy something, you say, "Hi, how are you doing." But the guy you deal with, who maybe even owns the business, may give the impression he barely wants to deal with you.

The best way to leverage existing clients is through your database. Regardless of how you got the sale, you need to look at ways of getting data from your clients. It can be as simple as getting them to fill in a questionnaire. That data is worth more than anything else to your business. It's worth more than your best salesman. You can break it down by date, the last visit, last spend, by purchase. They all give different angles to look at.

HOW MUCH ARE MISSING CLIENTS COSTING YOUR BUSINESS? SNATCHING THEM BACK MEANS... FRESH PROFITS!

Without question; one of the fastest ways to leverage that data is to look for lost clients. You'll find 60-70% of people who haven't come back don't really have a great reason not to come back. You can easily contact those clients and pull them back.

Send a private mailing with a great offer to a hundred or so miss-ing clients. Quite a big portion of them will come back because you've reminded them that you're there, you're a great business to deal with, and they were happy before they disappeared.

Just Ask!

Ask them, "Was there anything that we did wrong? If that's the case, can you let us know so that we can put it right?" Then make them a killer offer to get them back. Ten days later, send out a sec-ond mailing to the clients who didn't come back and increase the offer. In the third mailing, you take the offer right to the edge. Why do you do that? Because the question is, what's the lifetime value of that client? Do your maths and take the offer to the absolute edge. Believe me, it works because you're going to get 60-70% of those peo-ple coming back. What is that worth to you in a year?

THE FREE CLIENT MACHINE...
REFERRAL MARKETING

Here's another way. You know that you need more customers to walk through your door every single week. Do you spend cash in the press to bring new people in? Or can you leverage your existing cus-tomers? What you do is make your existing customer a great offer based on referral business. You make that offer known through posters, signs or flyers.

You can apply this to any business.

With our hairdressing salons, we used to have a referral system where we would say to the clients:

- "Are you happy with your hair today?" They had to con-firm that they were happy because some people won't tell you they're happy or unhappy.

- Then we'd say, "Will you do me a favor? Would you like your next service at half price?" Only an idiot is going say no.

- So you say, "I'm going to give you this referral voucher. I want you to put your name and address on it and find a friend who's going to use it and write their name and address on it. If they use it within seven days I'll do your hair for 50% off next time."

In twelve weeks, our stylists were completely packed out just by us using existing clients to build a business. We barely spent a penny on advertising!

You can get your clients to do that. Let's say you've got an evangelical customer who just loves you to death. They adore you and they will die for you when they're like that.

How much is that evangelical client worth to you if you do their service for free? They're worth a fortune based on the volume of business they bring into your business.

You say to this customer, "I love dealing with you and I know you love coming here. I'm going to do everything for you for free because I know this year you've sent me 40 new customers."

It's a piece of cake this stuff.

All you have to do is instead of looking out, you look inside the business. Just leverage the existing client to bring in new business.

A big mistake I've seen with a lot of businesses is that they do a kind of reactive marketing where they just try it and hope it's going to work. There's no sustained campaign, no plan of action. That's when it's going to start costing you a fortune because the returns will be virtually zero.

CALL THEM, EMAIL THEM, FAX THEM, JUST TELL THEM... WANT MORE PROFITS AND GROWTH? FOLLOW-UP!

Something I've done stacks of is getting people back in. Let's say, every six months your client has his Chevrolet serviced in your garage. But you look at all your statistics and say to yourself, "Hang on. These guys are actually only coming into the garage when their car breaks down or it's running really sluggish. The reason is they're not getting a service every six months, so how do we get them in?" Nobody wants their car to explode when they're driving down the freeway. It's just that most people couldn't care less about their car unless it breaks down.

So how do you remind them?

You send them some direct mail saying, "Hi, you've probably totally forgotten but did you realize it's now six months since you last had your car serviced. And it's at this point that most cars start to break down. It's at this point that the fan belt goes, you start using more fuel etc etc."

So you're kind of pushing them on into action. He probably would have his car serviced anyway. But you reminded him.

You can use this in anything.

You can remind people that you're the restaurant in the county easily. But people may get to Saturday and think, "Where should we go and have dinner tonight?" If you're using direct mail, you just remind them just to leverage that database. I don't care what business you're in. You can go right across the board with it.

Get ideas from different businesses as well.

Don't just look within your own business. Look at businesses that are completely unrelated to what you do.

PACKING AND STACKING; THE SALES VOLUME BOOSTER

For example, rather than buying a ticket for football for just one ticket at the gate, you can buy one for the whole season. What I thought was, "Hang on, these guys are selling a year's seats in advance. Even if these guys don't turn up." That's what they do in gymnasiums, as we know. People pay for these health and fitness clubs. But do they go? No they don't.

So what I started doing was selling a year's hairdressing.

We let them have a discount price and they would then have a season pass for the salon. It created a kind of slightly indifferent loyalty to the business because you're going to have occasions where they're not happy and want to leave. But then they think "Hang on, I've paid in advance for my hairdressing. So if I leave I'm going to lose all that cash."

At the same time, the advance ticket was based on a rewards system.

See page 10 for exclusive reader-only FREE offers!

Every six weeks they would build up their reward. And then at 18 weeks, which was their third visit, they could cash their reward in; they could get everything for half price or at the end of 36, they could have a color, or one of the big services for free. It was a good system.

Loyalty built into the season ticket worked very well.

The truth is though, that the best thing that we ever discovered in our business was, without a shadow of doubt, direct mail. Direct mail exploded that business from £60,000 a year to a quarter of a million, which is half a million dollars.

SLASH STOCK COSTS, INCREASE SALES VOLUME BY PRE-SELLING

I'll tell you what I did with another guy. He was selling prestige cars. Now what was really strange is that this guy literally had a room full of custom cars from donkeys years ago.

These cars went back for decades. We pay a lot for our cars in the UK so we can save quite a hefty sum if we import a car from Europe. The same car you can buy in the UK say for £20,000, you can probably buy in Europe for £13,000. The difference is pretty substantial and to import probably costs £1,500 to £2,000.

So it's a big savings.

These guys I did some work with thought well if they could bring these cars over to the UK and put them in our for call they could sell them at a killing and still sell them cheaper to the consumer.

So I said, "Hang on. Why don't you sell the cars before you actually order them?" This was a bit radical for them although it's nothing unusual.

Mining the database...

What we did was strip down their database and culled all the sports car buyers from a couple of years previous. I said, "What you need to do is make a big song and dance over the whole thing and let this database know that you're bringing this car into the country. These cars cost £31,000; they're going to be able to buy one from you for £24,000.

We'll say to them, we'll give you XYZ for your car based on

these criteria and this is exactly what it's going to cost you a month." We sold 18 before they even landed in the UK. It was just incredible - £1.2 million.

CONCLUSION

We've covered leveraging your client's network and contacts, upselling, building the relationship with your clients using direct mail and more. You need to know your clients and relate to them.

It's not difficult...

Some of these methods are obvious. I've given you plenty of ways you can quickly grow your business. Now it's up to you.

See page 10 for exclusive reader-only FREE offers!

FREE Offers, Unique Solutions And Valuable Business-Building Tools Exclusively From Our Team Of Co-Authors!

FREE!
Continue Your Learning And
Business-Building Online:
www.MDMSbonus.com

Never Closed a Prospect Before?

The Proven Closing Methods of Sales Mentor Susan Adams Will Immediately.... Boost Your Sales, Increase the Number of Customers You Close QUICKLY and Have You Getting Top Dollar for Your Products and Services.

There are few sales products that teach **Sales for the Non-Sales Person**. Most programs are targeted at the sales professional. People who already know how to close a prospect.

What about you--the Small Business Owner? Someone who needs their business to succeed? What sales products are there to help you take your business to the next level?

You need to be able to effectively talk to customers if you want to make your business grow. It also has to be easy. You don't have time to read endless books on selling, attend sales workshops or hire a coach.

Maybe you wonder if taking a basic sales course might be a good idea? Of course, those courses are usually a few days and can be several thousand dollars. You probably don't want to take the time away from your business.

How many times have you.....

- **Left a meeting without a signed contract?**
- **Never heard back from a prospect after a meeting —and don't know why?**
- **Sent proposals that never get a reply?**

Why Spend the Money to Market Your Business If You Can't Follow Through And Close The Sale?

To start closing more prospects and growing your business, please visit:

www.salesforbeginners.com or www.susanadamshome.com.

The Closely Guarded Secret That Will Increase Your Business By 100 - 300% or More ... Virtually Overnight

Dear Business Owner,

Do you know what the most powerful way of getting new business is? **Master this and your business will go through the roof.** The most powerful way to get NEW business is a recommendation from a CURRENT customer. The most powerful way to get new business is REFERRALS!!

So how do you get referrals? ... **GREETING CARDS!**

Let me give you an example. About a year or so ago we bought two cars, one for my wife and one for myself. The person that I bought my car from handed me his business card and that's the last I ever heard of him. I long since discarded his business card. I don't even remember his name.

The person we bought my wife's car from is Martha. How do I know this? Martha sent me a birthday card. She sent my wife a birthday card. She sent us a Holiday card. She even sent us a Happy One Year Anniversary of buying our car card! Last week my neighbor asked me where I got my car from. Who do you think I recommended? Martha of course!

Well Martha told me her secret! She uses an Internet based system that allows you to send Real Physical Greeting cards from the Internet. These are not "E-cards" but real Physical Greeting cards that arrive by first class mail! You can send hundreds of cards at the touch of a mouse. Upload photos, schedule cards to go out in advance, create custom cards etc. It's amazing!

Martha told me that since she started using the card system her business increased by 300%! Great News ... **I have arranged for you to try the system for FREE!** It's a great tool for Realtors, Mortgage Brokers, Insurance Agents, Sales People, Business Owners, Chiropractors, Dentists, Professionals etc. Anybody that has customers or clients and wants more business!

Ready for More Business? ...TRY IT FREE!

Visit http://SendCardsFast.com

Need Business Advice? ... Call Jack Bastide 800-595-2252

"More Million Dollar Networking Secrets You Won't Want To Miss!"

We hope we've encouraged you to go out and make some new connections.

In our chapter we established the basis of networking as relationship building. Everyone can do that, right? Absolutely. But knowing you can do it and actually carrying it out are two entirely different things. Sometimes we need a little nudge in the right direction.

That's why we created Network Mania Secrets. We want to help people like you ... people like us, really ... move forward in their networking ventures. We want you to see all the possibilities and not miss any of the opportunities. There's so much out there and our chapter only scratches the surface.

You see, everyone approaches networking differently. We interviewed over 20 mega-successful entrepreneurs to learn their secrets. And they revealed them.

There was no way to fit the flood of information into a single chapter. But we don't want to hold anything back, either.

We're working out the agreements with our co-authors, but for now you can get complete access to all the interviews. These are the "raw takes"... uncut and uncensored, not self-serving "infomercials." And we're still adding interviews.

But we can't guarantee how long your "backdoor entrance" will stay open. Head over to www.NetworkManiaSecrets.com/backdoor now, before we have to close up shop.

Everyone loves a good story. We love hearing how others have conquered fears or found success in strange places. We enjoy tales of unlikely heroes. Most of all, we like identifying with other people. We want to believe if they can do it, we can too.

Like the people we introduced to you in the chapter of this book. They took the steps to change their lives. And so can you! If you have a networking success story to share, email us at success@networkmaniasecrets.com

Don't Wait Until It's Too Late!

Sign up today and you'll be taken directly to the page where you can listen to David Garfinkel, Mike Morgan, Dr. Harlan Kilstein and many more share their Greatest Networking Secrets in their own words for FREE!

Name: [   ]

Email: [   ]

Say Yes to a brighter future...

Submit

**You'll find this exclusive sign-up at
www.NetworkManiaSecrets.com/backdoor**

Your Prospects Hate The Hard Sell. The Soft Sell Doesn't Work. Selling Today Means Gently Evoking Powerful Emotions

"Here's How a Canadian Talk-Show Host Uses His Secret Interviewing Techniques To Effectively Erase Resistance And Spark... The Buy Now Impulse."

My name is Shaune Clarke. Let me get right to it. If you want to make more sales...

You Must Get Intimate With Your Prospects - You Must Bring Out Their Hidden Emotions

This is no easy task. It requires careful attention to human psychology. Here's what I mean...

I'm a marketing consultant and direct response copywriter now, but I was a talk show host for many years. Great interviewers quickly build trust. They bring up deep emotion in their guests. To do so, I developed my own powerful strategy. I call it The Secret Six™. It's a specific series of questions, asked at just the right time, in just the right way.

This Same Process Allows Me to Dig Deep Into the Buying Psychology of Your Prospects.

Their hidden emotional desires are revealed. By focusing on these needs, in your sales copy, your prospects become far more responsive.

This is not common practice. Most consultants study demographics, review existing marketing materials, and then carefully predict what will motivate your prospects. Clearly this will not generate the most successful sales message.

By using The Secret Six TM we will uncover:

- The single most important thing you must say to instantly gain and hold your prospect's attention
- How to deeply connect and empathize with their problem
- Simple statements that instill trust and dissolve resistance

Prospects will feel good about buying from you. It's something they want to do, not something they feel pushed to do. One more thing...

When You Hire Me, I'll Interview You As Well. Here's Why...

Your one-of-a-kind experience is what sets you apart. Your personality is a customer magnet. These are dynamic sales tools to be strategically used in your sales message.

Let's put them to work. Here's how you can reach me.

shaune@dynamicresponsemarketing.com
Toll Free 1- 866- 486- 4884
You Can Get My Newsletter and 51 Point Website Checklist For Free at
http://www.DynamicResponseMarketing.com

At last!

A systematic way to get and use testimonials for maximum impact!

Want to get maximum mileage out of testimonials? Not sure how? The *PROOF PACKAGE* will help you to turn your testimonials from an anemic afterthought into a tactical tool of persuasion.

Here's what you'll get in the Proof Package:

- A complete list of **39 ways to use testimonials** in your marketing.

- **Testimonial dissection** - the exact elements every testimonial should contain for maximum effectiveness.

- **Feedback forms** that you can send to your clients requesting testimonials.

- **Sample release forms** to get permission to use the customer's testimonial.

- **Interview questions** to ask when interviewing your clients to get a testimonial.

- **Compliance Guide** - The use of testimonials is subject to regulation in some states and industries. Here's what you need to know to stay legal.

- **Quick Start Audio CD** - This audio talks you through everything in your Proof Package, and how to use it.

- **BONUS CD** - an interview with Eileen Coale, copywriter, about using testimonials and other marketing tactics, conducted by business strategist J.P. Maroney (approximately 30 minutes).

PLUS a very special BONUS SECRET for using testimonials to target customers in a whole new way!

For more information, or to purchase the Proof Package, go to www.proofpackage.com

Finally, the Secret is Revealed!

Learn how to Reclaim 70% to 90% of Your Lost Profits by Harnessing the Power of Repeat Sales

Back-end sales and the never-ending cycle of getting the customer to purchase your next item is probably THE **most important step** in any effective marketing campaign and the missing piece of the puzzle for most struggling businesses.

But it's not the ONLY step!

In our **"Small Business Marketing Fundamentals"** manual we reveal 101 "must-have" strategic marketing secrets for YOUR small business, including:

- The ONE **psychological perspective you MUST shift** before you will ever make the kind of money you want to make with your business!

- The **proven five-step formula** that must be a in every bit of marketing and advertising you do, otherwise you are just flushing money down the toilet!

- How to avoid the **"dumb things" that 9 out of 10 companies are doing** to lose their shirt with an ineffective Internet presence! (Caution! one of them may be YOU!)

- The secret to getting ONLY interested prospects into your marketing funnel, and how to make the right emotional connections with them **so they will buy again and again** without anyone having to sell!

- The secret to getting **500% greater response** than color brochures, business cards, and all other forms of product or image advertising COMBINED!

- The **simple 4-step FORMULA** unknown to over 95% of businesses that can increase your customer response by 300-600% or more!

PLUS, as a special BONUS, act now to receive these two special reports:

- **"13 Deadly Small Business Marketing Mistakes,"** and

- **"11 Secrets To Small Business Marketing Magic - How To Get More Business To Come To You In A Month Than You Now Get All Year!"**

Claim Your Copy Now at:
www.SoCoSolutions.com/SB101/

Get A Free Professional Review of Your Copy or Marketing Materials!

Claim your Free Review (a $197 value) Today... Enjoy Bigger Profits Tomorrow!

If you'd like to **make more profit** from your business... generate more sales with less effort... identify easy changes that can multiply sales... and **correct embarrassing mistakes**... this could be the most important page you read in this book. *Here's why:*

Worth More Than $197 - But You Get It FREE

I'll do a free review and critique of your marketing materials - based on my hourly fees, this is a $197 value.

Many who have taken me up on the consultation have told me that they were sure it was a marketing ploy, but discovered that it was worth far more to them than $197 - even if they did not retain my services. Why? Because I need to understand your business as a whole before I can even think about writing copy for you.

The process of getting to know about your business is quick (because I have learned precisely what to ask), and will be enlightening for both of us.

You may discover opportunities, challenges, and marketing methods you've never considered before.

Plus, Claim Your Free "Makeover Video"

I have put together a free video that shows me doing a makeover on a website for a real client. You can see the "before & after" and understand the reasons why the changes were made. You can even use the ideas you see for your own website without paying me a dime.

"This offer doesn't cost you a dime -- but it could multiply your sales, profits, and leisure time in ways you never expected."

To Claim Your Free Consultation
Call (800) 780-4345
Or visit: www.ConsultWithRay.com

Increase Sales Now!

For Entrepreneurs Who Have To Sell, Hate It, But Need to Make More Money Doing It

Discover an entirely new way of selling that takes the pressure off you and the prospect...and leads to prospects closing themselves

Free 30-Minute Video Will Provide An Instant Sales Increase

Let's face it - making sales in today's marketplace is tougher than ever. Competition has increased, so buyers have more control than ever before. In order to survive in today's market, your persuasion skills have to be razor-sharp. Anything less, and you will find yourself out of business.

The Strategic Marketing Coach Selling System™ eliminates many of the obstacles sellers face. The objections that currently stop you dead in your tracks will no longer be a problem, because when you use the system properly, the prospect handles his or her own objections. You will take back control of the sales call, and lead the prospect toward making a decision.

Get A Positive Outcome On Every Sales Call

You will get a positive decision at the end of every sales call. A positive decision will be a "Yes" or a "No," and nothing in between. Prospects won't tell you they want to "think it over." This means you can stop chasing prospects and start making more sales. This is a selling system that will give you back your life. No more spending your nights and weekends wondering what your prospect is going to decide.

Become A Selling Super Star

Once you use the Strategic Marketing Coach Selling System™, you will gain a new level of confidence in your ability to persuade, and you will go into every selling situation with no fear. You will expect to get every sale. Selling will be fun. Most of all, you will make a lot more money. Frankly, there is no better way to improve your bottom line than to improve your persuasion skills. Nothing else gives you a higher return on investment.

I invite you to learn more about the Strategic Marketing Coach Selling System™. Visit our website, and watch our 30-minute video training. If you are like most people, just viewing the video and applying what you learn will give you an instant increase in sales. You can also call me direct for a free 30-minute evaluation. Together we can determine if the Strategic Marketing Coach Selling System™ is right for you - without any obligation or expectation on my part. I look forward to visiting with you.

Ed Forteau
The Strategic Marketing Coach
www.StrategicMarketingCoach.com
Stanton, MI   866-835-9433

*"How to Write Mouthwatering Sales Copy…
Even If You Can't Write To Save Your Life."*

The "secret weapon" behind most of the top Internet and direct marketers shows you…

Dear friend,

Is your salesletter or website unproductive? Perhaps you want to write your own copy, or know for sure if the copy you have will indeed pull for you? If so, then listen up.

In this specific video sample, I tear down and rewrite the most important part of any piece of sales copy: the headline. This video is about 15 minutes long and, best of all, it's FREE.

Here are some of the powerful tips you learn…

- The worst place for a testimonial and one thing it should NEVER compete with (this website had it all wrong, and it's costing the owner sales!)…

- The one color that consistently outpulls any other color for the headline…

- "Swiping" is a good technique (duplicating an idea or style), but using an old, proven headline in this particular case was done all wrong, and why…

- Why using this specific word in the headline can scare readers away…

- The "hook" (or "unique selling proposition") is the most powerful element of the headline, but falls flat on its face in this particular critique…

- A few suggestions culled from the most widely read publications in the world that's proven to dramatically boost your readership…

- How to use suggestive words that provoke vivid mental imagery and increase your sales (along with a few examples to boot!)…

- A specific yet powerful tool that gets people in the proper frame of mind before they even begin reading the body of your salesletter…

- One simple trick that can crank up your sales by turning your headline into a grabber your readers will find irresistible…

- And so much more!

Go to www.TheCopyDoctor.com to watch this powerful video now!

To higher profits,
Michel Fortin
Copywriter

"How To Put Your Business On The Fast Track, Using Cost-Effective-High-Impact Marketing"

What is the difference between the businesses that grow, regardless of the market, the competition, or even the economy... while no amount of hard work seems to help others?

Having a well thought-out marketing strategy will put you on the right track... surer and quicker than anything else you can do for your business. Have you had a marketing strategy makeover, lately?

A complete marketing strategy makeover will help you identify the most effective ways to grow your business.
• Target your ideal clients.
• Reach them with powerful, compelling messages.
• Position yourself far above the competition.
• **Even build a business that will grow in value, on autopilot, without your constant blood, sweat and tears.**

If you cannot take a month or two off, and still be in business, you have to ask yourself:

"Do I Own My Business-Or Does My Business Own Me?"

As a marketing strategist and copywriter, John Gilvary can help you design and implement your optimal marketing strategies.

Strategies that will assure that you have a real business-one that you can sell some day. Most entrepreneurs wake up after years of owning their business; only to find that they really didn't have a business... they

bought themselves a job. A job that required working long hard days only to find that when you removed them from the business, there was very little left to sell, or leave to their loved ones, or create a retirement income for life.

All they had to do to make a difference is change a few simple strategies back upstream. Now is your chance to get a complete review of your current situation... and a preview of what you can expect downstream. The choice is yours.

If you want a full review of your business situation, including some additional strategies I didn't include in this book, I invite you to contact me, at johng@jgilvary.com. The first 100 businesses that contact me and mention this book will get their first 100 gift cards... free. Everyone will get the additional detailed descriptions of the remaining six ways to profit from using gift cards.

Are you looking for a dynamic speaker for your industry group or corporate function? John Gilvary has spoken professionally to hundreds of business and community audiences, with content customized to each group. Call John for the details.

John Gilvary
Castle Rock Publishing

925-418-8213 or toll free: 877-418-3390
www.jgilvary.com
johng@jgilvary.com

http://johngilvary.blogspot.com

Cutting Edge Online Shopping Cart Software
Provides An All In One Solution for
Your Small Business Problems

Generate Massive Online Profits Using GoldbarOne's Online Marketing Tools, Easy Site Integration, and Guaranteed 99.9% Up-Time

(You can even get 30 days free)

If you've wasted dozens of fruitless hours trying to make other online shopping carts and ecommerce solutions work for you... or if you've let other online shopping cart services ding your credit card for months even though you've never successfully used their shopping cart... or if you're just flat out technically challenged... then this may be the most important message you read during your entire online business career.

Hi, my name is Marc Goldman. My team and I built the GoldbarOne® online business solution after we had personally struggled to find an easy ecommerce shopping cart that would meet our ecommerce business and marketing needs. We paid thousands of dollars for online shopping cart systems that didn't work, were difficult to use, or failed to deliver on their promises.

That's why I stopped buying and started building. The result? GoldbarOne® — the only suite of online business and marketing solutions you would ever need to run your site.

It doesn't matter if you've already got a website or if you're thinking about starting a new one... GoldbarOne® can help.

Experts Who Do the Work for You

After running an ecommerce business since 1998, it has become very clear to me that most serious business owners have absolutely no interest in setting up their own online shopping cart, autoresponders, etc. — no matter how easy it is to do!

So while we take pride in the scope and simplicity of the GoldbarOne® ecommerce shopping cart, we recognize that serious business owners need (and want) something more. That's why we created ExpertOne™...

For a low monthly fee, not only will you get every benefit of GoldbarOne®, you'll also get direct access to our IT department — the same guys who built the GoldbarOne® ecommerce system.

They'll set up everything for you. They'll import your products and email lists, plug in any (or all) of the internet marketing tools you want to use, maintain everything, even send you monthly reports.

Accept This 30-Day Free Trial...
http://www.goldbar.net

Who Else Wants a FREE 44-Minute Marketing Consultation?

(Available Only to Readers of This Book)

Would you like to quickly discover easy marketing strategies that will make a significant, measurable impact on your bottom line? Or how about some simple tweaks you can make to your advertising that can boost response as much as 400 percent?

Call me today at 720-344-7788 to schedule your free 44-minute marketing consultation. I'll analyze your business, cut to the heart of your marketing problems, and show you multiple ways you can quickly bring in more customers and boost your revenue.

I normally give 29-minute consultations to people who visit my site. But because you've purchased this book, I'll give you 50% more time at no additional charge. You'll get a full 44-minute consultation during which I'll be totally focused on how to quickly and easily grow your business.

Now, there is a catch. Books live long lives, and I can't honor this offer indefinitely. So you must contact me by phone or email before the end of July 2007 to schedule your consultation. After July 2007, all bets are off.

To contact me, please call 720-344-7788. Or visit www.HealyMarketing.com and complete the form I've posted at the bottom of the page. Your answers will be immediately forwarded to my email address. Please allow 24-48 hours for a response.

I encourage you to pick up the phone and call me now. I look forward to speaking with you.

Ryan Healy

"Get the Makepeace Magic"

Clayton Makepeace's Proven Direct Response and Copywriting Secrets For Producing Bigger Winners, More Often - Free in your In-Box Every Monday...

Plus, "Beat The Blank Page Blues - 3 beginning outlines for every kind of copy you'll ever write" is Your Free Gift For Giving My E-Newsletter a Try!

Claim Your FREE Subscription at:
www.makepeacetotalpackage.com

If you're a business owner or marketing professional you think about it all the time... You can almost taste the sweet rewards that more successful sales promotions would bring you!

Heaven knows you're not asking for much - just...

Bigger Winners - A few tenths-of-a-percent lift - a mere 10, 20 or 30 more orders per thousand mailed...

More Often - Two or three breakthroughs like that a year - or better yet, five or six or more...

...and the sky's the limit for you!

• **If you're a business owner**, you'd get the unrivaled satisfaction of doubling, tripling, even quadrupling your sales revenues and profits ... seeing your product or service enrich far more people's lives ... and ultimately, of cashing out for a king's ransom.

• **If you're a marketing professional**, you could write your own ticket - to the big promotion, the huge raise, the choice corner office, and all the perks superstardom brings.

• **If you're a copywriter or marketing consultant**, new clients would cheerfully shower you with fat fees and truly obscene royalties ... pursue you, instead of the other way around ... and give you everything you need to make life great for yourself and your loved ones.

I say you deserve all of the above - and more. And I have a way to help you get bigger winners, more often, in just minutes each week!

Every Monday, I'll send you dozens of great ideas -- specific, how-to, nuts-and-bolts direct response marketing and copywriting advice -- all hand-picked by me to give you bigger winners, more often. And I'll back everything up with real-world examples, not hype and hot air.

My response-boosting secrets have made my clients more than $1 BILLION RICHER ... They've made me millions in royalties ... And now, they can help YOU grow richer, too!

If You'd Welcome the Most Highly Praised Direct Response Marketing and Copywriting E-Newsletter on the World Wide Web, Be Sure to Check Out *The Total Package*™ by Clayton Makepeace.

Claim Your Free Subscription Today:
www.MakepeaceTotalPackage.com

The Profit Center™ • Jupiter, Florida • 800-827-0940

Entrepreneur Magazine calls his strategies 'wildly generous' - now business growth strategist, award-winning speaker, and best-selling author JP Maroney - Mr. Monetizer - reveals the secrets behind...

Entrepreneurs Who Walk on Water

Discover why they're growing up to 9,721% faster than their competition!

PLUS:

- Discover a proven plan for building revenue 100%... 200%... even 400% or MORE!
- Easily DOUBLE your revenues in the next 90-120 days!
- 3 Common reasons revenues get "Stuck" (and what to do about them)!
- And a $500 Free Gift to Explode your revenue!

These entrepreneurs do the impossible.

While the rest of their industry ekes out single digit growth - they grow by 200%... 300%... even 1,000% or more!

Like:

- Dov Charney who's growing his American Apparel at 524.6%!
- John Marshall who's EveryTicket.com posted 3-year growth of 811.6%!
- Jon Yarbrough's Video Gaming Technologies of Smyrna, TN growing at the ASTOUNDING RATE of 9,721%!

While ordinary businesses feel lucky to get 10%-20% more customers in a year - they DOUBLE... TRIPLE... and QUADRUPLE their customer base in a single quarter!

FREE Report: "The Art of Profitable Growth"

Hi, JP Maroney here. And, I've put together a Special Report I'd like to put in your hands - TODAY! Claim your FREE report – and a FREE $500 GIFT by visiting:

www.JPMaroney.com/growfast

Questions? Call Toll Free 1-800-304-5758

Jason "Profit" Moffatt Proves…

Even Complete Rookies Can Get A Slice Of The Lucrative Internet Pie

www.TheNewbieBible.com

Starting an online business can be a bit intimidating when you don't know where to begin. Luckily for you, I have provided a simple, one-stop resource center for all your internet marketing needs. Within the Newbie Bible you'll get instant access to…

- Step by Step Marketing Videos

- Ground Breaking Audio Interviews

- Products That You Can Use and Sell Right Now

AND IT'S ALL FREE!

I have been blessed to learn from extremely thoughtful mentors online. They didn't charge me a single dime when I started out, and I am eternally grateful for this. In keeping up with the spirit of generosity and honest good-will, the Newbie Bible was created as a free resource to help anyone who wants to make some cash online.

The Newbie Bible is my gift to you. Please take advantage of the vast resources and internet learning tools at…

www.TheNewbieBible.com

Wishing you the very best,

Jason Moffatt
www.ProfitMoffatt.com
jason@profitmoffatt.com

Anyone Else Want to Explode Their Yellow Pages Advertising Response 200%... 500%... or More?

Here's what it takes to dramatically increase Yellow Pages Advertising call frequency and quality... and why your competition doesn't have the first clue!

It's the epidemic of Yellow Pages advertising.

Each advertiser looks at the competition for ideas for their own ad... the Yellow Pages design department continues to design a vast majority of the ads in their book. And so it goes...

Instead of standing out, everybody just blends in.

When you consider the level of competition you face in the Yellow Pages, that's "the kiss of death." Fortunately, it's easy to stand out when everyone else looks the same.

Imagine having an ad that jumps off the page... credibly convinces prospects that you're the best, most risk-free option in your category... and consistently delivers more phone calls, of better quality...

Drawing upon proven direct response principles, Alan Saltz has been helping Yellow Page advertisers - in more than 16 countries - make the transition from mediocrity to category dominance.

He uncovers time-tested secrets including:

- How to craft a winning headline
- How to jump off the page
- How to catapult your credibility
- How to combat skepticism
- How to get a prospect to act now
- And much more

It's all revealed in his best-selling tell-all guide, The Definitive Yellow Pages Success Course, backed by an "Iron-Clad, 365-Day, No-Questions Asked Money-Back Guarantee." It has been praised as "The Bible of Yellow Pages marketing," and "The holy grail of Yellow Pages advertising" and has met with rave reviews from business owners in dozens of industries. Get it now at http://www.YellowPagesProfit.com

---

How to Use Yellow Pages Advertising to Ethically "Steal" Business from Your Competition...

MENTION "MDMS"
& RECEIVE $50 OFF
YELLOW PAGES AD DESIGN

Visit: http://www.YellowPagesProfit.com
Contact: alan@YellowPagesProfit.com
Call: 877-243-9612

Two Crazy Ladies Inc.

Established in 1988, Two Crazy Ladies Inc. set out to provide a professional approach to empowering our clients to strengthen their relationships with their customers. Whether it is a strategic, operational or tactical requirement for corporately identified goods or programs, our team researches the best products to be properly aligned with corporate identity and goals, to maximize the marketing dollars spent on promotional items.

We are very proud of the reputation we have earned for being one of Canada's most innovative and idea oriented promotional companies. Our clients have come to depend on our "personal touch" approach to service and our absolute dependability. We continue to expand and improve our product lines and develop and maintain excellent rapport with our suppliers. This ensures that we will be able to take our clients' goals and turn their vision into a plan of action that results in a successful promotional or recognition campaign.

E-commerce On Line Stores, dealer and customer incentive programs, employee recognition programs, years of service programs, product launches, tradeshow giveaways, gift with purchase programs and so much more. Tell us what you are thinking, we'll tell you how to leverage premiums and logowear to extend your brand identity for any venue. 18 years and 100's of successful campaigns are our reward with customers such as Dell, Olymel, M.S. Society, LCBO, CH2M, CNIB, Palm and [yellow tail] rely on our expertise.

We can do anything you need!

Melanie Sibbitt
President / Owner

Giorgia Domingues
Director of Marketing

Two Crazy Ladies Inc.
604 Gordon Baker Road
Toronto, Ontario
Canada
M2H 3B4
t: 416-494-2244   tf: 1-800-735-2654   f: 416-494-2272
www.twocrazyladies.com

Alan Forrest Smith is an internationally acclaimed public speaker and writer. He has written copy for some of the world's leading entrepreneurs and businessmen and is a consultant for companies both in the UK, in Edinburgh, Manchester and London, and abroad, having been flown across the globe to countries such as Australia and Singapore to share his expertise.

A keen businessman since the age of 10 years old, when he started repairing bicycles for cash, Alan Forrest Smith is now focused on creating one of the biggest, best and most dynamic Advertising Agencies on the Planet!

Websites where you can see Alan Forrest Smith now are...

www.NonConformistMarketer.com

www.TheCopywritersMasterclass.com

www.MegaMasterclass.com